C O R P O R A T E

Voodoo

SINESS
AGICIANS

RENE CARAYOL and **DAVID FIRTH**

CAPSTONE

First published 2001 by
Capstone Publishing Limited (A Wiley Company)
8 Newtec Place
Magdalen Road
Oxford OX4 1RE
United Kingdom
http://www.capstoneideas.com

CIP catalogue records for this book are available from the British Library
and the US Library of Congress

ISBN 1-84112-157-6

Designed and typeset in by Baseline, Oxford, UK
Printed and bound by Biddles Ltd,
This book is printed on acid-free paper

Substantial discounts on bulk quantities of Capstone books are available to
corporations, professional associations and other organizations.
Please contact Capstone for more details on +44 (0)1865 798 623 or (fax) +44
(0)1865 240 941 or (e-mail) info@wiley-capstone.co.uk. In North America
please contact John Wiley & Sons for more details on 212 850 6000 or (fax)
212 850 6088.

Contents

Introduction

A message from René and David

Out of this world

Many Priests were either killed or imprisoned, and their shrines destroyed, because of the threat they posed to Euro-Christian/Muslim dominion. This forced some of the Dahomeans to form Vodou Orders and to create underground societies, in order to continue the veneration of their ancestors, and the worship of their powerful gods.

West African Dahomean Vodoun: Historical background
http://spiritnetwork.com

The word Voodoo means 'mystery'.

Voodoo was a secret – or rather was driven into being a secret by those who would rather it didn't exist.

Voodoo was access to knowledge, power and enlightenment that the majority – the establishment, those who were in a position of authority – did not have.

From the 1600s until the close of the eighteenth century, between 11 and 15 million black people were removed from Africa by the slave trade.

Voodoo was a way for its practitioners to get back to something natural, instinctual, reverential – something earthy and elemental, something with a bite and a rhythm and a groove to it, something hot, something joyful, something that would make you shout out loud, something that could transport you back home.

Corporate Voodoo offers a similar promise.

In the world

Life is a mystery.

Business is a mystery too. 'The old certainties don't apply', we were told so often by the gurus of the 1990s. Then the dotcom economy emerged and gave a huge, shocking glimpse of a world where the old certainties were not just inapplicable but blown away, really and truly blown away. And then, come August 2000, the dotcom bubble seemed to burst. But have we gone back to where we were, to what we knew before? No. We remain in a stressful, speeding world, breathless excitement and limitless possibility in one moment matched by breakdown, confusion and insecurity the next. It's a world crying out for peace and self-knowledge. The spirituality and self-help industry is on a roll. It's also, strangely, a world that is crying out for Magic. You'd think, after what we've all been through recently, we'd want things more certain. But no.

Mr. and Mrs. Dursley, of number four, Privet Drive, were proud to say that they were perfectly normal, thank you very much. They were the last people you'd expect to be involved in anything strange or mysterious, because they just didn't hold with such nonsense.
Harry Potter and the Philosopher's Stone, J.K. Rowling

The thing is, it's in the house. The strange and mysterious is in the house. The Dursleys, who resist life in all its fullness, are nevertheless the guardians of Harry, *wizard of great fame, someone who once conquered death and crippled a devilish foe.* The magic is with us, would we just see it.

Corporate Voodoo is the gateway to a magical world.

This book

This book is our way of sharing the 'secret' knowledge – natural, instinctual, risky, thrilling, scary – that a few people are practising today.

Let's join with Harry Potter and J.K. Rowling and call these people Initiates.

Their magic is a strange mixture, like Voodoo itself, of the old and the new. Initiates don't throw the baby out with the bath water, they don't have a modernist stance that dismisses any approach that was practised in the past. Their rule is: work with what works.

Initiates follow the magic and make their businesses Fast. You'll see what some have done in CHAPTER ONE (though don't expect anything that feels like A Chapter in this book – just go with the flow, just keep listening, just keep using your imagination instead).

People who don't have the access to the mysterious world of magic, let's call them Muggles.

Muggles end up making their businesses Slow (CHAPTER TWO is the sorry tale of woe).

If more Muggles became Initiates, what implications would that have for our society, for education and government? That's the inquiry of CHAPTER THREE.

But only part of transformation comes through the work of analysis and vision. *Corporate Voodoo* shamelessly offers pragmatic advice on what to DO.

How can you transform your company into a Fast one?

And how do you as an individual make the shift from Muggle to Initiate?

The two essential qualities that most separate Initiates from Muggles in our Voodoo world are their FEARLESSNESS and their attitude to OTHER HUMAN BEINGS.

Initiates of Corporate and Personal Voodoo are masters of two common human experiences.

They have a healthy attitude to failure, seeing it as rich in learning and opportunity. Muggles, on the other hand, engineer their efforts to avoid failure or the impact of failure, and thus compress their lives into what is known and predictable.

Initiates engage fully with life and all its surprises. They know that nothing – good, bad, failure, success – exists except as a label, a perspective of the mind, a point of view. Having faced fear as an ally, they are therefore grateful for the lessons of any experience. And they move on.

Muggles are scared of one thing more than any other: they are afraid of other human beings. And they hide that fear behind a show of power.

The history of organisations has been the history of subjugation, conformance, control and micro-management, not because of any scientific understanding that this produces the most efficient use of the human resource, but from a deep-seated fear of what might be produced without such confining approaches. If we stop drumming, will the rowers stay in time? What if we let people be different? What if we let people be themselves, rather than what we expect them to be?

But for now, listen up. Can you hear that music playing..?

Voodoo is suspicious of the neat and tidy answer

The Spell

Planet Earth...

It is the year – well, it is whatever the year is –

The technological revolution rages on.

New-world rebels representing the networked economy are besieging the old world with the most sophisticated weaponry ever seen.

The internet

As online populations continue to experience stellar growth, established corporations are being driven towards electronic business and new media strategies in a last-ditch attempt to adapt.

Old-world traders are being told 'destroy your business' and 'evolve or die' by the new rebel leaders. And all those who fail to respond will be mercilessly sacrificed in the new economy. Little regard is shown to the history of these dominant, commercial leviathans.

However, some of the new-world rebels are also falling from the skies – those who flew too close to the sun – exemplifying for others the new intolerance of recklessness and ineptitude. They are being sacrificed for the greater good.

Until now.

Voodoo loves
the mess

Until Voodoo...

... a new force and its guardians, sworn to uphold the visionary yet beautifully simple secret of the force, and to share its rewards.

The team will use the force to mentor, coach and convert old-world giants and headstrong rebel forces to fly in the new dawn.

The fundamental belief behind Voodoo is that the old world and the new can coexist and cooperate, by sharing the wisdom of experience with the energy and vigour of youth.

The power of Voodoo.

The Prayer

It is the first of November.

When you wake at last from your dream the image that haunted you then has not left you now.

A tall elegant man...black as the ace of spades...dressed in blue jacket, long white shorts with the name CANADA (for some reason) emblazoned in red around them, a Panama hat which has carried much dust and a devilishly debonair cravat of deepest purple...

...takes his cigar from his mouth...and peers over his sunglasses at you with cadaver's eyes.

But everyone around you is laughing, laughing, as this *oungan* – God in heaven knows where this sudden familiarity with the language has come from – bursts into electric life, now telling vulgar stories and vile jokes, now squaring up in mock fisticuff, now bending over to spread his buttocks – all maple leaves and the letters ANA – towards you.

And then someone over your shoulder, unseen but a comfortingly English voice this one, says 'Don't worry, old chap, he's possessed by lwa Gede, the lwa of the dead.

'They say that the eccentric behaviour of the Gede (such as you witness before you here) actually expresses turning death into satire. Imagine! Playing death in order to outwit it. That may be

Voodoo
inhabits harsh
reality
and Voodoo
inhabits the
dreamworld

their scheme I suppose. For if death is unavoidable – the universal outcome – outplaying it with life lets one face it successfully. Don't you think?'

And in your familiar bedroom on your familiar bed with your familiar partner asleep beside you, you make a brief calculation that, all being well, you have about 39 years left to live and only 16 of those with the company.

All being well.

The Great Crossing

Voodoo is probably the best example of African syncretism in the Americas. Although its essential wisdom originated in different parts of Africa long before the Europeans started the slave trade, the structure of Voodoo, as we know it today, was born in Haiti during the European colonisation of Hispaniola. Ironically, it was the enforced immigration of African slaves from different tribes that provided the circumstances for the development of Voodoo. European colonists thought that by desolating the tribes, these could not come together as a community. Torn from their families and their kinship groups, the slaves experienced a profound sense of alienation. However, in the misery of slavery, the transplanted Africans found in their faith a common thread.

> *...corporate voodoo connects people, releases people from the slavery of old ways of being, thinking about and leading organisations....*
>
> *...corporate voodoo is powerful...*

They began to invoke not only their own gods, but to practice rites other than their own. In this process, they comingled and modified rituals of various tribes. The result of such fusion was that the different religious groups integrated their beliefs, thereby creating a new religion: Voodoo, an Afro-Caribbean religion that mixed practices from the Fon, the Nago, the Ibos,

Dahomeans, Congos, Senegalese, Haussars, Caplaous, Mondungues, Mandinge, Angolese, Libyans, Ethiopians, and the Malgaches.

> *...corporate voodoo is a mixture, a compound, a brew of old and new, sensible and mad, sacred and profane. It works with what works, not what's acceptable...*

As they were distributed among the plantations, work groups and huts, the different ethnic groups were systematically mixed; in effect, slaves were meant to lose all memory of family, lineage and origins. Stripped of their humanity, they became easy to manage, primed for a life of total submission...But the strength that the Africans in Haiti gained from their religion was so strong and powerful that they were able to survive the cruel persecution of Voodoo by the French rulers. When the French realised that the religion of the Africans was a threat to the colonial system, they prohibited all African religious practices and severely punished practitioners of Voodoo with imprisonment, lashing and hanging. This religious struggle continued for three centuries, but none of the punishments could extinguish the faith of the Africans who kept their religion a secret.

> *...corporate voodoo connects people with what is important, meaningful and instinctual; it creates successful organisations – successful at the economic and the human level – because it works with what inspires and frees people...*

> *....corporate voodoo need not be a secret any more....*

It is in the dance that Vodoun touches most closely to the mystical, for every motion that the dancer performs is a magical metaphor for the invisible world, and it is no wonder that spirits arrive most often during the dance. For the divine recognises itself and is drawn into the eternal movement of the dance.

Voodoo asks: why clarify the contradictions?

And now let the dances begin to the sound of the drum...

to cross the great divide

to return to the source,

to remember

The all-night dance ritual is a memory that runs deep within us all; a memory that takes us back to a time when people had respect for our great mother earth and each other. Dancing was our rite of passage, our shamanic journey into altered states of reality where we embodied the Great Spirit and the magic of life.

We danced around great fires, we chanted and we drummed, empowering ourselves and our community. Then the religions of fear began to take hold . They destroyed our dance rituals, burning all who dared to question the new order. However, the power could not be suppressed forever and the great cycles of time have brought us full circle to this moment where we are gathering once again. The ancient memory has reawakened, the all-night dance ritual has returned.

At Return to the Source, it is our vision to bring back the dance ritual. A ritual is a sacred act with focused intention. We aim to create a modern day positive space, created with love where we can join as one tribe to journey deep into trance, just as our ancestors did.

We view the dance floor as a sacred space where we can connect with our power. To create this sacred space, we use totemic art and props, created by visionary artists. A large crystal is hung above a seven pointed star in the centre of the dance floor. The star symbolises the grounding of cosmic energy into the physical plane.

Dancing on symbols is an ancient ritual practice which allows the energy of the symbol to be awakened.

Sacred water from the Springs of Glastonbury, the spiritual heart of Pagan England is also sprinkled around the space and American Indian sage is burned to cleanse the energy. These ancient sacred acts give us positive energy, empowering our intention of the dance floor as a unified place of freedom and love – the 'source' of all that is. – **Chris Decker**

To connect with the power of rhythm means to expand awareness. – **Reinhard Flatischler**

Dance, trance and the ecstasy of life. There's nothing the human species needs to experience more today. – **Matthew Fox**

More than 4 million people go dancing in clubs and bars across the UK and Europe every weekend spurning individualism and materialism In pursuit of empathy and euphoria. The vast majority take E, speed, cannabis and cocaine whilst they are doing so, and then they come to work for you on Monday morning (they've got to have a job, you see, to have this much fun).

They park their car in the usual place, maybe, maybe not, and check their personality in at reception.

By about Tuesday afternoon their body will have had its first chemical backlash against the Es they took at the weekend and they'll be feeling uneasy and slow, though you'll barely notice.

And then you sit down with them. And you tell them a story. A story about work, jobs, organisations and the world of business in this the first decade of the twenty-first century. {Please, they really don't care if 31.12.99 or 31.12.00 was the eve of the new millennium; both nights were great party nights.}

So what is your story?

What is your story?

Maybe it's this...

Initiates create Fast business....

And you'd say:

Speed is the legacy of the age – but speed's not the same as Voodoo.

The business world is moving faster and faster. Maybe you notice that? Maybe you don't?

Maybe you're only used to the way things are – and that because you've no slower age to compare it to, you don't think that it's any faster nowadays. They say that if a cloud were sentient – that's a weird thought isn't it? – it wouldn't notice the effect of being blown about in the sky because it has no grounding, literally, to base the comparison on.

The major legacy of the internet era will be speed. You'll have heard this before. Technology has invaded all of our lives, and life will never go back to the old pace. The new generation of young business people don't think that technology is moving fast enough – do you? – whilst many still fear the advent of this ever more complex technology driven world.

Do you?

But it is not just about technology; it is about a different generation of leaders and entrepreneurs who are more courageous, challenging and ambitious: the Voodoo leaders.

The major legacy of the internet era will be Voodoo. That you won't have heard before.

This new cadre of Voodoo leader is exemplified in the New Economy and dotcom companies which

Voodoo asks: do you know what you're doing?

exploded on to the scene throughout the 1990s – the Jim Clarks and the Marc Andreessens of Netscape, the Jeff Bezos of Amazon and the Jerry Yangs of Yahoo! But there are many so-called traditional businesses which have grasped some of these new attitudes and have delivered spectacular results on the back of this movement. Think Carly Fiorina at HP. Think Jack Welch at GE.

The key driver for the emergence of this new form of business leadership was the stellar growth in valuations of internet and technology stocks throughout the late 1990s.

And what else? What else made the world a fertile ground for this Voodoo world? The cult of the individual post Reagan and Thatcher; greed; a demand for more, now, by everyone; a higher standard of living; the peace dividend; changing values in society; the rise of the self-sufficient, latchkey-kids; generation X workers; the growth of self-development, spirituality, health and well-being as an end in itself; more TV channels; raised expectations of a better life for everyone. And some world-shattering, newly exploited, technological advances.

The possibility of changing the world for real (unlike the hope that your parents' Peace and Love movement would change the world) and the promise of joining the world's largest legal wealth creation system created a gold rush not seen since the Klondike days of the nineteenth century. Similar to the gold rush era, this drive for 'explosive valuations in months' left many casualties, and some spectacular winners. Some first movers were left face down dead in the hard earth. Others stepped over their frozen bodies to make their way to the gold.

It is worth taking some time to look at some of the beneficiaries of a bold, aggressive, impatient leadership approach: the Voodoo way.

Let's use a few examples as our starting point.

GLIMPSE OF VOODOO 1: **VODAFONE**

Only a few years ago British Telecom (BT) sat at number one in the FTSE 500 as the largest company in the UK by market capitalisation. It had scale, financial muscle, a captive customer base, and a regulator who appeared to be on the BT payroll. It was inconceivable that throughout the ensuing shake-up of the telecoms sector that BT would ever be toppled. At this time Vodafone was still a division of Racal. Vodafone at the time was one of four relatively new and small mobile phone operators in the UK. BT had pitched in with Securicor to deliver Cellnet, which had tremendous reach and advantages, given its parent companies. Orange and One to One were new fast-moving entrants. Vodafone has since blown the competition away, and is now the largest wireless phone operator in the world and, by some distance, the UK's largest company. Orange has been bought and sold a couple of times and is currently heading towards another capital event by a flotation. These transactions have generated some £30 billion for its shareholders, with more to come. And Orange is still to deliver a profit!

Voodoo loves New Age financial engineering

How?

We will look more closely at BT in the next chapter, as their fall from grace has been just as spectacular as the rise of Vodafone and Orange.

Voodoo is risk-embracing

So what of Vodafone? Their key weapon has been a real visionary and combative leader in Chris Gent. He has embraced growth and scale on a global basis as his key measurements of success, and has been single-minded and aggressive about achieving these. Vodafone has benefited from having negligible baggage, and being able to hire and nurture its own Fast business gene pool. They have been extremely customer facing, and have worked very hard to communicate on a regular basis with customers. This has not been 'right first time' – but they are good at not making the same mistake twice. Through innovative use of novel financial instruments they have built the financial resources to go on a not-before-seen acquisition run that has seen them dwarf their competitors. This has made them the talent magnet of the sector (unlike BT, who appear still to be appointing only from within, which would lead one to ask: where are the new ideas coming from? But more of that later).

Gent has flown in the face of accepted wisdom. He has attacked on multiple international fronts. Change has been a necessity, not something to fear. Vodafone is very comfortable partnering on many fronts, as long as this delivers the returns and growth that such a large organisation will need to deliver to shareholders. Whilst others have still been working on their strategic plans, Vodafone have been executing good enough strategies, and recruiting great people, and moving them through the organisation at a pace commensurate with their contribution. They have grown their infrastructure with some slick deals utilising experts via strategic alliances and partnerships, very different from the old school of 'we only make, we never buy – no one can do this better than us'. In the new world of business, building everything yourself just takes too long, and most organisations do not have the requisite talent or leadership to do it all.

VOODOO LEADER **CHRIS GENT** – Vodafone Giant

Chris Gent is the Chief Executive of Vodafone Group plc, a position he has held since 1st January 1997.

Chris joined the Vodafone Group as Managing Director of Vodafone Limited in January 1985 when the mobile phone service was first launched, and held the position until December 1996. He was appointed a Director of the Vodafone Group Plc at the time of its initial public offering in 1988, when it was known as Racal Telecom plc. The company changed its name on the total demerger from Racal Electronics in 1991.

Prior to joining Vodafone, Chris was Director of Network Services for ICL. In this role, he was Managing Director of Baric, a computer services company owned jointly by Barclays and ICL, and was responsible for ICL's computer bureau services worldwide. He also held several positions at Schroder Computer Services. He began his career as a management trainee with National Westminster Bank in 1967.

Chris has many interests, including playing tennis and watching cricket. He is a former National Chairman of the Young Conservatives (1977-1979). At the time of leaving ICL, he was Vice President of the Computer Services Association Council.

Voodoo loves virtual

An essential plank of Fast businesses is their ability to be 'virtual' (they don't own all elements of the production process or the supply chain). They are not just comfortable with this approach, they consciously use it as a key part of their armoury. What really separates Gent from his competitors is his courage and his desire to embrace risk in a manner that many of his fellow leaders in this sector just cannot imitate. His stealth attack on Mannesmann was an object lesson in eyes-out assault and nerve.

The attack changed the corporate landscape in Europe. Before the Mannesmann deal Vodafone had already created America's largest wireless business with a deal with US telecom operator Bell Atlantic. It now had more than 28 million customers worldwide, including 10 million in the UK, and posted a 113% rise in profits when the last results were announced. The takeover saw the creation of an international telecoms giant with 54 million customers in 25 countries and across five continents.

The Vodafone chief has been said to combine persuasiveness, affability, guile and determination. While he said "I am not a ruthless shark," at a press conference in Dusseldorf, launching the hostile bid for Mannesmann, one friend recently remarked that "he never does anything that isn't calculated." — **Vodafone — from *Racal to Riches* by Stirling O'Rourke**

Days before the final bid for Mannesmann, Gent told reporters: "It may be unprecedented, but it's not unachievable."

Interview with TWST.com

TWST: *What else would you say are your company's advantages, and who and even what do you see as your competition at the moment?*

Mr Gent: In terms of competitive advantage, in most of the markets we operate in, because of the speed with which we've accelerated growth, the way we've managed and stimulated usage, and our focus on costs, we tend to be market leaders with lowest cost infrastructure to support our customers. That's very important because the tariffs keep coming down and we bring them down in order to broaden the appeal and to stimulate usage. So we have the advantage of our scope and scale giving us even better opportunities to procure equipment and services at lower cost. And we intend to continue that process. We can offer our new scope and size, offer new services which will differentiate our offer from our competitors, who tend to be isolated in any one country, for instance, BT, our competitors in the UK, Deutsche Telekom in Germany, France Telecom in France. Those companies are getting their act together to cooperate and compete, they find it extremely difficult both culturally and for reasons of commercial objectives. So we believe that what we've done is make a major step into a competitive advantaged position which will be very difficult for others to copy or to compete with.

Voodoo asks: are you thrilling yourself today?

GLIMPSE OF VOODOO 2: **ORANGE**

Orange may not have the scale of Vodafone, but with the flamboyant Hans Snook as Chief Executive Officer, they have built a fast-moving, innovative culture that is focused on building value. They have probably the most exciting brand in the sector. Wally Olins, Chairman of the branding giant, Wolff Olins, is still excited by the thinking that went into the establishment of the Orange brand. "They understood clearly what their major customer franchise would be; they wanted the young and the 'young at heart'". Snook saw the potential for stellar growth of mobile communications across Europe. His competitors were competing and communicating technology, scale, reach, price and service. Orange successfully built a brand at previously unheard-of speed with a simple and universal message – OPTIMISM.

Voodoo loves optimism!

Orange launched as the first recognisable consumer brand in mobile telephones, and with an iconic advertising campaign. It also challenged the way in which users were charged, introducing per-second billing. It has regularly topped the rankings for signing new customers.

Snook's mantra is customer service – the key, he believes, to winning and, equally important, retaining customers.

Orange wanted to be seen to be the contemporary brand of the sector, not necessarily the biggest, and in their own way quirky. Many of the larger (and usually ex-state owned) European telecom behemoths have arrogantly believed that they could run this exciting but relatively small company better. This has led to huge valuations attached to Orange and the fabulous wealth earned by its management.

Both these excellent telecoms companies have eschewed the usual financial strait-jacket of a single-minded focus on the profit and loss account, and gone for growth. This has been done in the main through tremendously brave leadership, and the ability to attract and nurture a new breed of manager. And, let's not forget, slick New Age financial engineering. This new availability of capital has been one of the major drivers of change in the new economy. Apart from the advent of a huge number of venture capitalists who are keen to invest in these fast growing new entrants, the Chief Finance Officers and Financial Directors now have available to them many different alternatives to the profit and loss accounts and balance sheets to fund expansion and growth. What about securitisation against future earnings? How about a rights? Bonds, perhaps? Try a vast array of loans with differing risk profiles from a variety of different organisations? Flotations? Joint ventures? And so on. Show us the money.

As Snook stands down from his executive position, it's important to note that he'll still be engaged by Orange in an advisory capacity – i.e. focusing on 'vision and branding' (not, you'll note, on finance: there'll always be enough people – like his number two, Graham Howe – to take care of that).

This is what makes Snook a Voodoo Leader...

VOODOO LEADER **HANS SNOOK** – Orange Renegade

Like the visionary architect Howard Roark in Ms Rand's *The Fountainhead,* Mr Snook saw his career as a constant struggle against corporate mediocrity and state bureaucracy. Orange's original ambition was to be everything that British Telecommunications, the privatised former UK state monopoly, was not.

Within the British mobile phone industry, he put himself in danger of being stereotyped as a free spirit with a taste for *feng shui* and colonic irrigation. Mr Snook may have shed the ponytail, but he showed no sign of conforming just because his business was suddenly worth £31bn.

"The more the business has grown, the more confident he has become about expressing some of his more unusual interests", explains one colleague. In any case, the image belies a shrewd business brain. Orange's position as the UK's fastest-growing operator has been achieved through skilful promotion of its brand. Marketing is elevated above almost everything else and the management are far from casual when it comes to the company's public image.

There is an earnest side to his character, too – a stark contrast to the affable charm of Vodafone's Chris Gent. Mr Snook really believes mobile phones will change the world; were it not for share options variously estimated at up to £100m, it would be easy to believe he was motivated entirely by idealism.

Source: ft.com

Hans Snook has, perhaps unkindly, been called a faded hippy in the twilight of his years. But then he has also been dubbed the greatest visionary in the mobile telecoms industry.

© 2000 Reuters Ltd.

And yet...

The Orange flotation flop continued on the second day of trading as 1.3 million private investors in Britain and France watched helplessly as institutional big-guns drove the shares some 12% below their issue price. — **©Associated Newspapers Ltd., 14 February 2001**

Ah, well. Voodoo accepts uncertainty. Whatever...

Orange founder Hans Snook, in a statement released yesterday, said: "My own belief is that in the years to come, people will look back and marvel that they did not see more clearly the growth potential, which we have only just begun to exploit."
Guardian Unlimited © Guardian Newspapers Limited 2001

So there we have two Voodoo stories, Vodafone and Orange, from the telecoms sector. Gent, all cricket-loving and huge almost-impossible Capital Events and Snook, all self-realisation and brand evangelist.

Meanwhile, here's another person who's not afraid to push the self as brand...

GLIMPSE OF VOODOO 3: **VIRGIN**

It is not only in the technology marketplace that we have seen excellent examples of Voodoo initiates creating Fast Businesses. Virgin is worth a mention here. When Richard Branson briefed his Virgin Airlines management team that they were going to go against the world's favourite airline, amongst others, the first Virgin Atlantic jet left Heathrow 13 weeks later!

How? By creating a real virtual business where most things, including planes, were leased or delivered through astute partnerships. They have always had a focus on understanding the customers' requirements and being able to deliver this whilst others are procrastinating – sorry, performing their cost/benefit analyses.

Voodoo asks:
Why predict the future when you can make it?

Voodoo is open-cultured

Virgin are prepared to buy in talent right up to senior executive level. Their risk-embracing culture is well understood, and consequently they do get some things wrong, but this is a necessary part of winning and being Fast. It is hard to describe Virgin Trains as a success. It is interesting to note that, unlike many other Virgin businesses, the trains were not built up from scratch. They inherited rolling stock, staff and a poor reputation along with all other train companies. Given the choice, one would not want to start building a Fast business from here. One needs to understand that courage is not necessarily the absence of fear. Perhaps train companies will never be Fast!

VOODOO LEADER **RICHARD BRANSON** – Virgin Territory

Branson's brand is now brandished by some 220 largely autonomous companies. Often, he has a partner. Here's a sampling of his holdings—good, not so good, and unusual.
***Newsweek International,* June 19, 2000**

HITS

Virgin Atlantic The group's cash cow with 16 destinations worldwide and profits last year of £117 million

Virgin Megastores About 150 or so entertainment stores in prime locations worldwide, including Times Square

Virgin Direct Phone-based finance with 300,000 customers, now going online as Virgin Money

MISSES

Our Price Records Branson calls the British chain the 'most expensive problem ever.' Soon to be relaunched as 'v.shops'

Virgin Rail Poorly performing British railway franchises probably got the brand too soon. New high-speed trains promised next year

Virgin Cola Launched in 1996, the business lost £4 million last year after a further dip in sales. Still far from its original goal of overtaking Pepsi

HIGHLY ORIGINAL THINKING

Virgin Limobikes The coolest way to cross London: a fleet of motorbike taxis fitted with onboard passenger phones and radios

Virgin Bride Branson wore a gown to promote his big wedding shop in London

© *2000 Newsweek, Inc.*

Build brands not around products but around reputation. The great Asian names imply quality, price and innovation rather than a specific item. I call these 'attribute' brands: they do not relate directly to one product – such as a Mars bar or a Coca-Cola –but instead to a set of values.
Richard Branson

GLIMPSE OF VOODOO 4: **TESCO**

The retailing triumph of the 1990s was Tesco, reinventing itself from being a rather tardy but respected retailer that appeared to compete only on price. It had become accustomed to the number two spot to the supermarket champion of quality and value, Sainsbury's (which will feature in the next chapter). Under the stewardship of Terry Leahy, Tesco has changed itself and its image in a very short space of time. Leahy saw that customers had increased choice and price alone was not a sustainable competitive advantage, as someone will always come along and sell it cheaper. A much better competitive advantage was to have a good understanding of your customer base. Tesco's entry into the loyalty card business has transformed both their business and the supermarket landscape. They are now very much aware of who their customers are and what their spending habits are. This customer DNA has been put to phenomenal use. All stores are increasingly stocking what the local clientele would like to purchase and – importantly – not having to stock what is not required.

Voodoo says: The loyalty is in the data is in the customer

Despite the advent of Wal-Mart into the UK, and the blitzkrieg attack of the discounters, Tesco is still well ahead of the pack. They too have acquired a reputation for recruiting and retaining the best talent.

For an example of the confidence they have in going out to attract this talent, see the Appendix.

Meanwhile, let's have a look at what Tesco did to become a Fast business.

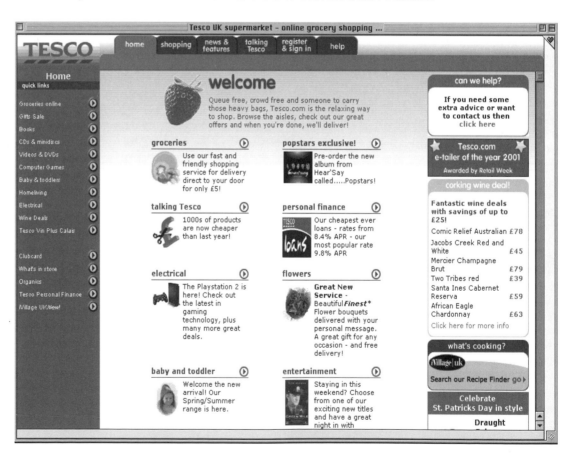

The biggest grocery service in the world.

Tesco corners the online grocery market

By **Darren Dodd** in London

Published: February 1 2001 07:36GMT

The UK online grocery market will be worth over $9bn by 2005 and while the US will remain by far the largest market at $32bn, Tesco, the British supermarket chain, is set to retain its place as the world's largest online grocer.

Datamonitor's report, *Exploiting eFMCG Opportunities,* says the UK has the most developed online retail market of any of the countries analysed, including the US. This is partly due to British consumers being used to giving credit card details over the telephone and so easily adapting to online ordering.

But apart from Tesco, few online services in the UK have yet managed to cover their operating costs. Smaller rivals such as Budgens have even pulled their online services. Budgens' failed venture cost the company £2.5m ($3.7m) in launch and closure costs and trading losses when it folded in September.

Other UK chains such as Waitrose are experimenting with a wider range of delivery options.

Tesco's online sales for 2000 are expected to be about $311m, according to the report. The company has been successful in winning new customers rather than cannibalising existing sales. It said in November that about 40 per cent of its internet shoppers were not Tesco customers before.

Nick Gladding, author of the report, said Tesco had enjoyed the advantage of a much earlier start than its competitors. The service is now almost six years old. Its business model, based on pickers taking stock from regular Tesco stores, had proved to be extremely successful so far.

Mr Gladding said that as the service grows the company would probably move towards a system based on a centralised and dedicated fulfilment centre. Other UK chains, such as J Sainsbury, Tesco's nearest rival, use a mix of in-store pickers and large storehouses to fulfil their orders.

Source: Ft.com

Voodoo says: the fundamentalists haven't heard the good news yet

Voodoo disturbs the way things are

Perhaps the best example of a Fast business created by that Voodoo blend of experience and bravado has been Tesco's entry into the internet food shopping market. All the major supermarkets in the UK have in some shape or form endeavoured to deliver an e-business channel to market. It is interesting to understand their differing motivations for entry. Some were driven by fear of new online entrants eating into their market share. Others were driven by the desire for the sizzle provided by an internet strategy and the consequent impact on share price and valuation, trying to catch the late 1990s e-fever. What Tesco's competitors also used was traditional thinking and risk-averse management steeped in the corporate culture. This led to a plethora of working parties, five-year plans, and significant investment in physical depots, warehouses and complex logistical strategies. These all take time and provide no learning. Tesco decided to test the water as soon as possible and started delivering orders received through their Tesco.Net website from stores local to the customers. This meant they were up and running in a few months. They have attracted some top talent from both within Tesco and externally. This exciting mix of experience and expertise has delivered a £300m business and accounts for over 70% of online food shopping in Europe.

Voodoo is customer-led

All companies that are successful – Tesco is no exception – face a risk. Success leads to a certain reluctance to change in response to a world which changes rapidly around us. In our competitive industry the penalty for misreading the customer for even a short time can be massive. Every successful business – small or large – must have both the willingness and the ability to change. Everything, if necessary, as the world around them changes.

It's not just the Internet, of course. We have introduced pharmacies staffed by fully-qualified chemists; full ranges of beauty products; books; newspapers; we are challenging manufacturers in the courts who are trying to prevent us from selling their branded products. We are offering banking services, loans, insurance policies, the lot.

All of this is driven by one thing, and by one thing only: our obsession – and I don't use the word lightly – our obsession with providing the customer with what he or she wants. I truly believe that Tesco spends more time than anyone in retailing in listening to customers, finding out what they want and finding a way of providing it. And we have to be at the forefront of technology to deliver what the customer wants, when, where and how he wants it. Customers' lives have changed a lot, their needs have changed – and we have changed out of all recognition in order to be there to respond. We are truly a reflection of the changes in society.

Our industry is customer-driven. And this has implications for planners also. The truth is that customers choose the kind of shopping they want to do. They love to be able to drive to a store with a big enough car park where they can wheel their purchases to a car, rather than trying to lug it all on to a crowded bus. That won't change and demand for the service is a long way from being satisfied. But: a lot of people do live or work in city centres and would like a store just around the corner from their home or office. Hence our hugely successful Metro format. Others like the idea of popping in to the garage for a few things while they fill the car up. Hence our Express developments with Esso. Some people even like to shop in the middle of the night: and we're open now for them too. Many would use a bus if they could, that's why we spend millions a year providing hundreds of bus routes to complement public provision.

British Chambers of Commerce Conference 2000
Extract from speech by Terry Leahy, Chief Executive, Tesco

Voodoo asks: how radical are you being this year?

And if you truly value your customers, maybe you should buy the people who help you know your customers most...

Tesco uses UK marketing company DunnHumby for its customer marketing and loyalty initiatives (the D&H tagline: 'no one wants to know their customers; they want extraordinary commercial results'). Their 'truly creative analysis' of Tesco's sales data brought the retailer a magical, Voodoo-like blend of both simple and obvious information to their fingertips. Don't sell bottled water in Edinburgh – the tap water's so good no one will bother with it. But do sell Caribbean haircare products in Brixton – funnily enough, you'll find a big demand for them there. D&H's work allowed Tesco to focus on the affluent and busy stores for the home delivery market – the customers who would not flinch at an extra fiver on the weekly shop to have it brought into their kitchen. D&H's work launched the hugely successful Loyalty card – and turnover has increased 51.6% since Clubcard's inception in 1995.

And then D&H wanted to float. Why not? Things were going well.

And so Tony Leahy – noting that Tesco accounted for a whopping amount of D&H's turnover – took a 51% stake in them.

'That's my competitive advantage', he thought, surveying Sainsbury's and the rest trailing in his wake. 'And you can't have it...'

On 10 April 2001 Tesco announced £1 billion profit for the year.

The voodoo initiate's spell again: fast!

The key attributes of Fast businesses include:

◆ **the ability to be virtual**
 – not having to own or build the components of the business. Time to market and first prover are far more important.

◆ **openness to recruiting talent from outside, even at senior management levels**
 – attraction of talent is seen as the key to their future. Loyalty is important, but contribution is vital.

◆ **close proximity to the customer**
 – understanding the customer DNA, and believing that fundamentally all customers have (increasing) choice

◆ **courageous and risk-embracing leadership**

◆ **think BIG, act small...**

> *Is that what you'd say?*
> *Is that the story you'd tell?*

Voodoo asks: when was your last life-changing moment?

You watch Giga – why DO they call him that? – arrive and take his seat amongst his colleagues over in the Content area

– all black army clothing, pockets and belts, hair stiffened and spiked, eyebrow piercings protected from the gaze of the corporate policy police by a couple of sticking plasters

– head nodding both to acknowledge the greetings of team mates and at the music still beating around his head through the 'phones attached to the mp3 player tucked in his backpack

and you think: got to keep open-minded, got to be more tolerant, got to keep open-minded, got to be more tolerant of those who are not like me

A picture and some accompanying words are loading themselves on your screen...

The idea that certain rhythm patterns or sequences serve as conduits for spiritual energies, linking individual human consciousness with the gods, is basic to traditional African religions, and to African-derived religions throughout the Americas. And whether we're speaking historically or musicologically, the fundamental riffs, licks, bass figures, and drum rhythms that make rock and roll can ultimately be traced back to African music of a primarily spiritual or ritual nature. In a sense, rock and roll is a kind of 'voodoo' . . .

Robert Palmer, *Rock & Roll, An Unruly History*

The arrival of African slaves has had one of the strongest influences on North American music. In the seventeenth and eighteenth centuries, millions of African people were taken as slaves to the U.S. to work on plantations in the South. They brought many of their own traditions with them but were forbidden to play their drums.

Louise Tythacott, *Musical Instruments*

African-based drumming, singing, and dancing, discouraged and repeatedly banned elsewhere in North America, had flourished [in New Orleans] since the early eighteenth century. This unique heritage has informed and enlivened New Orleans music ever since, as well as distinguishing it from the rest of American musical culture, making the city an ideal incubator for a nonmainstream music as rhythmically oriented as rock and roll.

Robert Palmer, *Rock & Roll, An Unruly History*

Today's drummer differs but little from the shaman in his incessant beating out of a rhythm, and likewise often enters into a form of trance while performing.

David Tame, *The Secret Power of Music*

One simple guideline for Christian music is NO DRUMS! Tambourines maybe, but NO DRUMS! CHRISTIAN MUSIC SHOULD FEED THE SPIRIT — NOT THE FLESH! CHRISTIAN MUSIC SHOULD EMPHAZIE THE MELODY — NOT THE BEAT!

Posting on *Hong Kong Association of Christian Music Ministry* Website

You bring another Search Results page to the front of your desktop and find:

HARRY POTTER: A new twist to witchcraft

This page is for those who seek the truth about the book series Harry Potter. Many think it is just harmless fantasy. True it is fantasy, but it is laced with witchcraft and demonology as are most books like it. Many say it gets children reading books who never would do so. I give you this thought. If your child did not like to take medicine and you had a chocolate drink with the medicine, plus arsenic in it, would you give it to them? You would if you did not know it was in there and what arsenic was. It is the same scenario with fantasy especially when it is laced with the poison of witchcraft.

Also look at the Satanic 'S' on Harry's head shown on the book cover.
Then look at the Satanic 'S' on the signs and symbols page.

The whole purpose of these books is to desensitize readers and introduce them to the occult. What a better way to introduce tolerance and acceptance of what God calls an abomination, than in children's books? If you can get them when they are young, then you have them for life. It's the oldest marketing scheme there is.
http://www.exposingsatanism.org/harrypotter.htm

If you can get them when they are young, then you have them for life.

You stare at the screen for a long time.

Then at last you click on the 'disconnect' button

and pick up the large envelope on your desk from amongst the scattered papers, empty coffee mugs, unopened books, drying marker pens, and maze of computer leads which represents the accumulation, the detritus of another day's work (though the detritus, to be honest, is actually yesterday's work..)

The report inside the envelope is headed:

Voodoo challenge: write your own most compelling story about you

Muggles live in slow business....

Muggles live in Slow business
Report prepared by **René Carayol,** *CEO The Voodoo Group*
Date: 21/2/01

You barely register the synchronicity

And it says:

We really enjoyed our meeting with you last week and our conversations with you about Fast businesses that are applying what we call the Voodoo spell.

We thought it only fair that we follow up with some examples of companies who are failing to make the magic work.

There are many examples of mature traditional businesses which have become 'veritable institutions'. They tend to be household names and no one would ever imagine a world where these stalwarts are not around. The key facet of the New Age Economy may be speed – and Voodoo – but many of our grandest institutions not only have never seen the need for speed to beat off the competition – they have for far too long been sheltered from fierce, fast moving competitors in their markets.

This has all changed. The change has not happened overnight, yet many large, complacent behemoths have not seen it coming. The late 1990s and certainly the new millennium have seen them put under pressure from all angles.

The Voodoo is not in the cornflakes

At The Voodoo Group, we've had the opportunity to either work closely with or study these old giants. There are quite striking similarities amongst them. One of the most concerning features of the majority of these organisations is that they were the market leader in their served markets, and in some cases massively ahead of the competition. This dominance has bred an arrogance and complacency, which has now borne the fruits of serious and potentially life-threatening failure. It is essential that these organisations understand and accept the reasons for their current hardship, and look to lessons of the New Age Economy for salvation. It is no surprise that their inherent culture has not enabled them to accept their deficiencies and more tellingly, the incumbent management are not able to turn these massive ocean-going liners around.

It is instructive to look at the attributes that have led to their current malaise. The uniformity of their problems is quite striking.

Voodoo is not: closed-cultured

The first issue for these companies is their impenetrable closed cultures. Companies of this kind

◆ have strong cultures which demand conformance, and do not tolerate mavericks or those who would 'rock the boat'. Consequently, they

◆ have low staff turnover rates. This has been seen as a great strength, especially amongst long-serving senior management. They have grown up within these institutions, and fundamentally believe that they have the only successful and sustainable method of winning in their marketplace. Until recently, history would have supported this view. However, in recent years the chickens have come home to roost.

◆ are beginning to recognise the need for change. Shareholders are increasingly concerned at their inability to respond to the new demands of the marketplace.

◆ have elder statesmen in the organisation who find it impossible to dance to a different tune. And tellingly, the next layer of senior management has also been gathering its corporate air miles for far too many years.

◆ need new ideas, new impetus – and new people. The old Voodoo spell of 'we grow and nurture our own gene pool and the best talent is home grown', is now proving to be the recipe for impending doom. A corollary to this is that the maverick talent they need will not want to join what they see as a constraining, conformist culture.

Organisations of this kind have a method of working which is epitomised by incremental improvement: doing the same things, but trying to improve and refine them over time. But when in need of a sea change, incremental improvement is just not radical enough.

Voodoo knows a bit of Latin (Radix [radical] = Root)

A key example of what a closed culture might do to you can be seen with Marks and Spencer (M&S). They were regularly voted Britain's most admired organisation. They were the UK's leading retailer for many years, and achieved this position through a variety of different economic measures: turnover, market capitalisation, sales per square foot, profitability – you name it, they were number one in their sector.

There was no perceived way that they would ever be toppled – but it's happening. The great green and gold giant is now struggling, and is increasingly looking like a target for acquisition. Having posted record profit results of over £1bn only a few years ago, it is in ruinous shape. The then Chairman and Chief Executive, Sir Richard Greenbury – the deliverer of those sparkling results – was forced to leave the business not long afterwards. This led to an unseemly scrap for the CEO's role. Keith Oates threw his hat into the ring, but was defeated by colleagues who preferred the homegrown stewardship of Peter Salisbury – another M&S lifer. (Perhaps he was still seen as an outsider by his board colleagues, despite over 15 years with the organisation?)

Voodoo hates jobs for the boys

Salisbury's mantra of radical reform and culture change fell on deaf management ears. They only knew one way to operate: the old way. His was not an organisation that appeared to encourage challenge or new ideas. It could be argued that it had far too many layers of audit-based management that spent its time checking on the layer below, NOT attempting to add value, vision or inspiration. This is an excellent structure for stability but a poor one for change. Mr Salisbury could certainly motivate his people to run faster, but he could never get them to run in a different race, even at snail speed. The major issue was that M&S, badly hurt by falling revenues, seemed to the market to have little idea or experience of what race to enter them in. Eventually Salisbury summoned up the courage to bring in some talent from outside at senior levels. However, these new incumbents appeared soon to be indoctrinated into the M&S way of doing things. Perhaps those who tried to challenge the status quo were treated with suspicion and not allowed into the inner sanctum.

M&S were brilliant at recruiting talent from the much-vaunted 'milk round' of the universities. They rightly prided themselves on paying top quartile salaries. They developed comprehensive training programmes for this new talent, who were in the main employed for their personal attributes, including self-sufficiency and the ability to challenge and be radical.

BUT:

The training programmes did little to sustain the radical thinking in them, and at the end of these programmes newcomers dressed and spoke like the rest of M&S management. The loose cannons that could have delivered the much-needed new ideas were brought into line by the prevailing culture.

This is not to say that M&S management are poor performers. They manifestly are not. What they are, are great implementers of someone else's decision-making. The whole management structure was built and honed to serve the directors of the organisation, who in turn were serving and performing for the CEO.

A much-repeated, self-inflicted wound was the approach to cost cutting in times of poor financial performance. The first items to be slashed were training budgets and graduate recruitment. Therefore any chance of breaking the mould or bringing in new blood would be lost. In times of crises, the only tactic was to run even faster, in other words: do more of the same. All this meant was that eventually they would be threatened with extinction even quicker!

Compare this story with that of another retail outlet: Dixons.

Voodoo asks: how are your strengths your weaknesses?

Dixons has been a stalwart of the high street for many years. During the 1980s it was an electrical retailer that specialised in cameras and photographic equipment. The longstanding Chairman and fulcrum of Dixons, Sir Stanley Kalms, has not just moved with the times, he has stayed well ahead of them. Dixons had a 'stack it high, sell it cheap' reputation much like Tesco did at the same time. Kalms's audacious move to acquire high street rival Currys introduced his huge ambition to his rivals. Dixons have been consistently innovative, aggressive and bold, but usually within the confines of their products and their served markets. In September 1998 we saw Sir Stanley's boldest and most risky move to date: Dixons launched the UK's first serious Internet Service Provider (ISP). This is worthy of note and admiration in itself, but his real killer move was to offer the ISP service for 'free'. This spectacularly aggressive move was seen by some as reckless and wanton.

Dixons were smart enough to know that such a different business would require a completely different culture. They gave Freeserve its own management team with its own Chief Executive. Dixons' decision to have an arms-length relationship enabled Freeserve to move at relative warp speed. Within two years Freeserve had been sold for £1.6bn, just before the real dotcom meltdown began. They have launched the successful new brands on the high street, The Link and PC World. The innovations machine is alive and well at Dixons. What next from the man who has all the attributes of Fast Businesses, coupled with his huge experience in this field?

Voodoo is not: product-obsessed

The second issue in Slow businesses is fixation with product.
◆ The 1970s and 1980s saw the massive advent of brands. Corporations were branding and re-branding on a phenomenal level, with some fantastic successes.

◆ The rather lazy shopping habits of the consumer meant we bought what we understood and recognised. Many consumers were happy to pay a premium for brands that were trusted to deliver what was promised.

Pepsi knew how trusting this consumer really was. The contents of a can of Pepsi-Cola hardly cost one penny, yet the brand building and associated marketing spend was quite phenomenal. Pepsi seriously knew how to market, and their customers never baulked at the premiums they were asked to pay. This was not just a soft drink to quench your thirst; this said something about your lifestyle. Pepsi drinkers were young at heart; they were seriously hip and fun. They wanted to be seen with their Pepsi.

This strategy worked brilliantly for a number of brands and their owner organisations for a very long time, and many of them are still trading successfully under these auspices today. However, the advent of the New Economy entrants into marketplaces dominated by the traditional businesses has created massive flux. The new entrants tend to have little baggage and no sacred cows. They are aggressive and prepared to take risks; this means they are prepared to make mistakes on a scale that has not been seen before by the management of their traditional adversaries. Simply speaking, the incumbent management in traditional organisations do not know how to cope with these upstarts who do not have years of brand identity to protect. The strong sage view of the traditional stalwarts was initially to ignore these fly-by-night companies – how could they possibly challenge their market dominance?

Over the past few years we have seen the birth and explosive growth of:

◆ BSkyB
◆ Next
◆ Matalan
◆ Virgin Atlantic
◆ Egg
◆ Vodafone
◆ Tesco.com.

They have built brands that are now extremely well known, perhaps even household names. They all have reputations for being very close to their customer base, and most have set new standards for service in their industries. They have the perception of being still new and young. They have made many mistakes and have achieved many startling successes. These are the new Voodoo captains of industry.

What was not quite understood was the impact they would have on the consumer. This impact would totally transform the marketplace. These insurgents were prepared to win by any means necessary. They would compete on price, service, experience, quality, anything. They were desperate for the customer. Many of these new entrants competed online, but not all of them. They were new, they were courageous, but most of all they were fast. The discount clothing retailers, like Matalan, were new and ferocious foes. They could move extremely quickly. They made mistakes, but learnt rapidly and secured sustainable positions in just a couple of years.

The real lesson learnt (for those who could learn), was that customers have choice. They were no longer just consumers, they needed to be treated like discerning customers who perhaps did not always know exactly what they wanted, but they were prepared to try different products and, importantly, from a wave of brands that were new, but exciting. These new experiences started to educate the customers about what they did not want. However, the only organisations that benefited from this feedback were those who were taking the time to listen. The New Age companies were so focused on the customer that they picked up this growing promiscuity long before the relatively out-of-touch traditional businesses.

John Lewis is a sad example of where a strong traditional business has clearly lost touch with its loyal customer base. The credit card is not a recent innovation, and many adults and teenagers are far more comfortable carrying credit cards rather than large amounts of cash. It is quite breathtaking that John Lewis only introduced the mainstream credit cards into their stores in the year 2000. What was it that led them to believe that they were meeting their customers' needs by not allowing them to pay for goods in the manner that they felt most comfortable with? Stunningly, they announced their decision to at long last accept credit cards as one of their innovations! Perhaps they should have apologised for years of what could be seen as contempt for their customers. Even then the change to cards was poorly thought through, and it was clearly a response to falling sales. They had no means of dealing with this innovation electronically; consequently they installed the manual carbon paper-based devices, which in the main had disappeared from the high street years before.

The parallels between John Lewis and M&S are clear. They appeared to act as if as long as products carried the John Lewis logo, customers would flock to the stores and buy them in

Voodoo asks: when was your last life-changing moment?

heaps. They had forgotten many years ago how to engage their customers, and certainly never appeared to listen to them. The John Lewis brand when compared with fast-moving, hungry new entrants, looked decidedly old and stuffy. They continued to sell the same things in the traditional colours. They persisted with the same methods of selling – or rather, said one insider, "We stocked the goods which were to be purchased in our stores". Customers bought. John Lewis would never want to be seen to be 'selling'!

Customers outside in the real world (and on the real high street) were beginning to encounter two alternative experiences. One was great customer service with new entrants (e.g. Gap) or same old mediocre customer service but at lower prices which better explained the lack of a premium service (e.g. Kwiksave, kids' clothes in Asda).

This inability to perceive that customers have choice is a major symptom of what we call slow businesses.

But Voodoo never loses hope. Even as this report is compiled, we read:

All change on Oxford Street as the mecca of sensible middle-class shoppers undergoes a multimillion-pound makeover

By **Robin Stummer** and **Hester Lacey**
25 February 2001

John Lewis, the destination for sensible shoppers seeking everything from curtain poles to tapestry kits, is about to enter the late 20th century. Its motto 'never knowingly undersold' has not been enough to stop a profits slump, so the company is to embark on a £13m revamp of its flagship department store in London's Oxford Street. The facelift is part of the deeply traditional firm's £300m strategy to expand and modernise its 25-strong string of shops that has already seen it break a decades-old taboo by hiring high-profile image consultants.

At the end of the Nineties, Selfridges, John Lewis's Oxford Street rival a short walk away towards Marble Arch, itself underwent a radical revamp – a massive building project that was hidden by a giant, wrap-around photograph of semi-clad models by Brit Artist Sam Taylor-Wood. Things will be different at John Lewis. While other, more flashy retailers undergo facelifts as a matter of routine, the John Lewis makeover – the first major change at the branch in 40 years – has all the gravitas of a state occasion (and no nudes). According to its managing director, Peter Still, the shop will become a 'retail theatre'.

The Independent

But then, don't all desperate organisations move the deckchairs around (their stores, their logo, their org chart) as if that might change their essence?

Voodoo is not: physical

Traditional, Slow businesses have another similarity; they are very physical.

◆ Things need to be owned or controlled by them.

◆ Whatever it is, they want to be able to see it and touch it.

◆ They are generally distrusting of elements in their supply chain or in the organisation that they cannot hold and control. This means that they tend to have suppliers and rarely have partners or joint ventures.

◆ They dislike out-sourcing because nobody can do it better than they can, no matter how far it is removed from their core competencies. An example of this is that they tend to have massive in-house IT shops that will endeavour to build everything. They rarely call in the experts, and will spend millions building systems that are readily available 'off the shelf'. Whitbread once built their own e-mail system!

Slow businesses are usually very late in adopting new technologies, and are far more comfortable allowing the competition to burn their fingers first. The strong view was that technology was just a temporary advantage. This view would have had a ring of truth, if the businesses could then swiftly adopt any new technology as soon as it was proven to work. However, slow businesses don't implement, they test. And they test in very labour-intensive and desperately slow ways. They test new tools and techniques to destruction. As a result, Slow businesses hardly ever catch up.

There are too many examples of sunk costs which eventually have to be written off, usually because in the years they have been developing and preparing for launch, the market has changed, and the 'new' initiative is obsolescent prior to its implementation. We have recently seen Budgen's having to write off its online food business. We have seen some supermarkets scrap their loyalty card schemes in the wake of Tesco's loyalty land grab.

Perhaps it is in the field of IT that most of the Slow businesses have really demonstrated that caution means sloth and waste. Governmental departments, with their frugal budgets, have been in the slow lane of change for many years now. They have to be public about their spends and projects. There has been a shameful litany of failed IT projects at tens of millions of pounds. The recent £70m scrapping of the Asylum system was nothing new; NHS, ambulance, Social Services had similar problems – the list goes on. The government departments are not alone. Banks, insurance companies, retailers have all experienced and tasted their constantly rising IT costs. Failures in the private companies have been kept low-profile, but there are many clues as to what's been happening behind the scenes. Many of our high street banks, we strongly suspect, still have not implemented e-mail systems!

Here are two case studies of what happens when slow businesses want to be physical:

◆ M&S decided that they needed a replica disaster recovery site for its Stockley Park data centre. Many organisations had opted for disaster recovery services from external organisations who would have the spare capacity to support the replication of systems should any disaster occur. M&S decided to provide its own. At one of its distribution depots in Hayes, Middlesex, they built a recovery site for Stockley Park only later to close it down,

Voodoo says: take care of yourself

when the true cost of this ultra cautious approach was really understood. It was never called into active service.

◆ Waitrose, the supermarket subsidiary of John Lewis, has a strong reputation for building all their IT systems themselves. There are many reasons for a company adopting such an approach, but the idea that 'nobody could do it better' is not one of them. M&S also wrote all their IT enterprise systems in-house for exactly the same reason, coupled with the feeling that they were particularly unique and nobody but they could understand how they operated. They also gave the oldest chestnut excuse: 'not wanting to be held over a barrel by any supplier'. Partnership is still not quite there yet: they prefer suppliers (having suppliers means you still get to hold on to the physical stuff). However, they are now held in a vice-like grip by their in-house IT function. They stuck with their 'supplier' of choice, which has, it could be argued, a particularly miserable track record of delivery.

This wanting to own and touch meant that huge amounts of capital were tied up in the Slow companies' hard physical assets like offices, warehouses and large IT mainframes. In the meantime, the faster moving competitors of these Slow businesses were leasing these services – going to providers who were experts in their field. It was the providers who would have invested in the latest technologies, or would have many buildings housing call-centre staff. This comfort with the virtual ownership of service as opposed to buildings, people and management, meant they could focus on their core business and drive growth. It meant that the Fast businesses would not be sidetracked with running elements of the business that were better run by experts, especially in the start-up phases of their businesses. This created relative jet propulsion in comparison to the *rigor mortis* that had enveloped the slumbering traditional giants.

The organisations that struggled with this more than anyone were the retail banks.

National Westminster Bank was the clear market leader only a few years ago. The retail banks are habitual brand changers. Instead of engaging their customers to understand what they really want from a service, it seems that they believe that just by a quick change in logo or corporate colours, all will be well. How many times does your bank change its corporate livery?

The advent of direct banking has rocked the retail banking marketplace. The ability to contact your bank when and where you want to by the means of your choice – telephone, internet or television – has set new standards of customer intimacy. The traditional banks have just continued to focus on size and scale, coupled with very fat profit margins and the apparent privilege of banking with them. This merger and takeover frenzy has led to enormous duplication of banks in the high street who are working in the same group. This, coupled with the enormous cost of running a physical bank branch, has encouraged many of the banks to rationalise the number of branches they have, with no thought for or consultation with their customer base.

This has led to uproar from customers. To demonstrate just how out of touch they really were, most of the retail banks decided to charge customers for withdrawing their money from cash dispensers. Many customers started voting with their bank accounts and the industry was forced to back down. This fixation with the physical assets has allowed new entrants to gain a foothold by offering the appropriate service to many disaffected customers of the banks, having asked them what they required first.

NatWest signals defeat, urges shareholders to accept Royal Bank of Scotland bid

AP – 11 February 2000

National Westminster Bank PLC gave up its battle for independence Friday, urging shareholders to accept a takeover bid from Royal Bank of Scotland PLC.

NatWest said it had become clear that a majority of its shareholders would accept Royal Bank's offer, which values NatWest at about £21billion.
"The board considers that it would not be in shareholders' interests to remain as a minority in a company that was no longer independent. Accordingly, the board now advises those shareholders who have not done so to accept the offer by The Royal Bank of Scotland," NatWest Group said in an announcement to the Stock Exchange.

Shareholders had not warmed to a rival bid by the Bank of Scotland, which had moved first against NatWest with a hostile bid in September. Royal Bank made its first offer in November.

The merged bank will have 15 million customers and be the third–largest in Britain in terms of market capitalization. Nat West chairman Sir David Rowland said: "We congratulate Royal Bank and look forward to helping them ensure the success of the new organisation."

One adviser to RBS criticised the NatWest board for not having recommended the offer earlier.
"We are obviously very pleased, although quite frankly it was inevitable. It would have been more graceful of them to accept three days ago," he said. A spokesman for the main finance union, UNIFI, said: "We want to talk to the Royal Bank of Scotland as a matter of urgency about its future plans.

"In particular we want reassurances that there will be no compulsory redundancies.

"We want to talk to them about constructive ways of managing the process."

The union fears that up to 18,000 jobs could now be at risk.

"It's time to show some leadership," said one investor. "They've done little enough for us in the past."

NatWest – as it is now known after another re-branding exercise – appeared to lurch from error to error. Its mainly home-grown talent was just not flexible enough to meet the more enterprising smaller banks who were growing rapidly with new products and services based around virtual ownership and delivery. Their banking networks were going up in weeks, not years. After prevailing over long-term share price erosion, NatWest were eventually bought by the Royal Bank of Scotland, who only a few years before were a relatively small regional player.

Voodoo is never: deeply cautious

The last attribute that these slow-motion experts have in common is caution.

◆ They live in constant fear of failure. This is a terminal condition in a competitive marketplace with agile new entrants who are entrepreneurial. One could imagine that many of the boards of directors in these Slow businesses have an imaginary 'too difficult' box in their boardrooms for the difficult decision-making that demanded an element of courage. These decisions would be put off until they were no longer relevant, or the subject had been fatigued out.

◆ These slowcoaches would dominate their board agendas with problems and issues in the organisation. They would tackle this right down to the smallest level of detail, thereby disenfranchising the management or operational teams who should have been dealing with them. Is this the best use of the board's time? Who was focusing on growth? Who was challenging the competition? Who is identifying the future talent the organisation would need?

◆ Boards that focus on futures and innovation tend to be far more courageous. The executives of any business must be comfortable with change. Change can be very difficult, and it forces rethinking and new methods of behaviour in order to master the new processes associated with change. Some businesses are comfortable with living with necessary ambiguity, for a time. Others would rather perish the thought.

Not that many years ago, the recently privatised telecoms giant, British Telecom, was head and shoulders above all other British-based telecoms outfits. It had been given a scale and infrastructure head start through privatisation, which was seemingly unassailable – or so we all thought. It was the largest company in the UK by market capitalisation and boasted of earning hundreds of pounds a second. With all their assets, they were set to be a dominant global player. They were given a customer base to die for. If you were going to start a new business, it appeared foolhardy to select the telecoms sector and come up against this immovable giant. But immovable it was. It appeared paralysed with fear. So much market share, so much revenue, and so many customers. The management felt the only possible way was down, so best to do nothing. The status quo was great. Thank you very much.

With all the firepower anyone could wish for, BT headed blindly into choppy waters, where they have been given the run-around, not by any one major competitor, but a whole flotilla of fast-moving launches which are picking off bits and pieces of this once huge empire. The Empire has been threatening to Strike Back for years. Competitors were nearly deafened by the din of the sabre rattling. And then,

– suddenly –

nothing happened.

This state of fear has continued with only the noise of failed joint ventures, profligate spend, huge debt and a sinking share price to accompany it. Vodafone has gone from nowhere to three times the size of BT in just a few years. Yes, British Telecom has also rebranded itself to become BT. Sir Iain Vallance and Sir Peter Bonfield, Chairman and Chief Executive respectively, have presided over this organisation for far too many years now – or so the press regularly suggests. The company is as sure-footed as Frankenstein's monster: in many respects it is the government's own Frankenstein. It also promoted for far too long from within. Peter Bonfield was quoted as saying that he has never moved a director against his wishes at BT. There's leadership for you! Who is taking the tough decisions?

BT is still sliding and will continue to, as long as it remains so cautious. Bonfield points out that all telecom stocks have suffered over the past year. True, but BT shares have underperformed in the telecoms sector by nearly 30% in the past 12 months. If anyone ever has the right environment in which to become comfortable with failure, they do. Unfortunately, it has now become a good friend of theirs.

Voodoo disturbs the way things are

BT dials old boy network to get successor

By **Chris Ayres**, *media business correspondent*

TUESDAY SEPTEMBER 26 2000

BRITISH Telecom plugged itself into the old boy network yesterday to find a new deputy chairman, after Lord Marshall of Knightsbridge said he would step down from the position next year.

Lord Marshall, who has faced criticism for the number of part-time directorships he holds, will be replaced by Sir Anthony Greener, the former chairman of Diageo, the drinks group. Lord Marshall continues to hold part-time positions on the boards of BA, Invensys and HSBC.

It is thought that Sir Anthony was recommended for BT's deputy chairmanship by Keith Oates, the former deputy chairman of Marks & Spencer, who is a non-executive director of BT and Diageo. Mr Oates, who announced yesterday that he would also leave BT, was given his job at Diageo – formerly Guinness – by Sir Anthony five years ago.

The management shake-up at BT comes amid troubled times. Its shares, which yesterday rose 15p to 750p, trade at less than half their value at the start of the year. Investors have hoped for a change in management for some time, but yesterday's shake-up is unlikely to satisfy them.

Sir Iain Vallance, BT's chairman, said: "[Sir Anthony's] vast experience in managing major international organisations will be invaluable to BT as we continue both to expand our global activities and to complete our transformation into a new wave Internet and multimedia business. I am particularly pleased that Sir Anthony has agreed to become BT's deputy chairman."

In response to Sir Anthony's limited knowledge of the telecoms market, one analyst quipped: "Perhaps someone who doesn't know anything (about the telecoms industry) is a good choice, given the mess that the people who do know something about it are in." Sir Anthony is 60.

So there you are: four attributes of Slow businesses, four qualities that Voodoo avoids. Learn from these Slow companies – what they have become is inevitable for them, given their conditionings and backgrounds and leadership. But it does not have to be that way for you. Remember:

◆ open the culture to internal and external influence

◆ out-source everything that's not core to your identity; in-source experts in what you can't do

◆ act with courage, act big

◆ treat the customer relationship as sacred

And don't get depressed by the size and age of these Slow businesses. I know you shopped in many of them when you were young, and your parents still like to think they'll be great again. Mourn them and let them go. It doesn't have to be that way:

◆ For every Slow business, extrapolating the past in terms of business structure and philosophy, there's a St Luke's blowing the past apart to reinvent the future

◆ For every company obsessed with the physical, there's a Visa, everywhere and nowhere

Voodoo
celebrates

♦ For every product-obsessed company, there's an Amazon or a SouthWest Airlines, branding, amazing, delighting

♦ For every organisation paralysed by caution and control, there's a GE and a Dell, pushing back the boundaries of what's possible…

It is your choice!!

As you put the report down, you notice that the computer has automatically redialled and found its way back to your original search results.

MUGGLES

'Fascinating! Ingenious, really, how many ways
Muggles have found of getting along without magic!'
– **Arthur Weasley**

'Bless them, they'll go to any lengths to ignore
magic, even if it's staring them in the face...'
– **Arthur Weasley**

'Muggles' are non-magical people in the parlance of the Wizarding World. Muggles are for the most part oblivious to the entire society of magical people which exists alongside their own. Part of the reason for this is that Muggles simply don't believe that magic exists, which means they find non-magical reasons for the things that happen to them. Another part of the reason is that the Ministry of Magic works very hard to keep the Muggles in the dark. When a Muggle sees a dragon, for example, the Ministry sends operatives to use Memory Charms to make the Muggle forget all about it. The Ministry hides some wizarding places with Muggle repelling charms; this is why Muggles don't see Hogwarts for what it is. Many Witches and Wizards look upon Muggles kindly, but some see Muggles as nothing but a nuisance and a bother. The Ministry enforces a Muggle Protection Act to ensure that all of the Wizardling World stays securely hidden from Muggle eyes. To most Witches and Wizards, Muggle society is essentially unknown. When they try to act like Muggles, the results can be humorous indeed. Hogwarts teaches a class called Muggle Studies where students learn about the ways that Muggles live and how they survive without magic.

– from **The Harry Potter Lexicon** *www.i2k.com*

Voodoo is not
found in the
kitchen at
parties

"...the lives of many kids are appallingly concrete – all wrapped up with test scores, TV merchandising, and mall trips – but my child still knows and appreciates the world of wonder and imagination. And that makes him and millions of other Harry Potter readers a bit abnormal, as Harry's mean uncle, Mr. Vernon Dursley, would say. In our culture, worth and meaning reside in things that we can count, measure, and accumulate. Even our dreams – like those of Mr. Dursley, who yearns only for business deals and a vacation home in Majorca – aren't concrete. No wonder J.K. Rowling calls us 'Muggles', people without a drop of magic in our blood."

– Jean G. Fitzpatrick, essay on beliefnet.com

Perhaps it's too late for your organisation, you think.

But what could we do about the next generation of companies?
Or about the next generation, full stop. What about the children?

If you can get them when they are young, then you have them for life.

Towards a Voodoo world: honour the children

Voodoo values
the vibe

In your hotel room that night, you flick vaguely through the channels, and eventually alight on the Business News on TV where the American announcer is saying

"and Steve Tice has been checking it out..."

Your TV screen pans over a TV studio set

[voiceover]

LONDON – The studio is set up to tape an interview show, *Pass the Mike* (as in microphone). The familiar tools of television production are in place. Thin metal beams overhead support spotlights, and dark, sound-muffling curtains encircle an audience of 40 or so people seated on wooden bleachers. Two cameras are pointed at cushy chairs on the tiny stage for the host and interviewee.

The members of the filming crew are in position: some wear headsets, some carry clipboards, all wear black T-shirts with white lettering reading 'BBC'.

This is not the British Broadcasting Corporation but the small production facility of Ladbroke Grove in a tough section of North Kensington, London, not far from the briefly famous Notting Hill neighbourhood.

The T-shirts are donations from the giant corporation to a small nonprofit organization named Youth Culture Television, or YCTV. The entire crew and most of the audience are teenagers, and the guest is none other than Mick Jagger.

YCTV is half skills center, half sanctuary from the mean streets outside. Most of the teens at YCTV (ages 11 to 20) are out of school, whether dropped or kicked. They may have failed in or been bored by traditional academics, messed with drugs, gotten pregnant or been in trouble with the school administration or, in a few cases, the police.

Ladbroke Grove was hastily converted from an automobile showroom in 1994 to provide a home base for the fledgling organisation. The brick building was carved into one studio with an L-shaped gallery above, three editing suites and several offices.

Jagger is not the only famous person to offer himself up as guinea pig for these novices. Over the last few years, Anjelica Huston, Harrison Ford, George Lucas, Dan Aykroyd, Bill Murray, Iman, Jeremy Irons, Sir David Frost and Jerry Hall have dropped by the studio. Many of them have been persuaded by a very persuasive woman named Sabrina Guinness.

Guinness, 45, founded YCTV and is its director. She is related to the world-famous brewing family but quickly points out that she has always worked and is not rich.

From the mid-1980s until 1993, Guinness lived in Los Angeles while working in the film industry. She saw first-hand the results of the 1992 LA riots, when much destruction was caused by teenagers who felt they had nothing to lose. Soon after that, CityKids, a New York organisation offering training in music and dance to inner-city teens, started a branch in Los Angeles. Guinness saw the group produce real change, and she hatched the idea of doing something similar in London.

Central to YCTV is the idea that if young people, especially those in trouble, are given a chance to prove they possess something important – creativity – they can do amazing things. Music, dance and, at YCTV, television provide natural outlets for this creativity.

Guinness believes television must do more to realise its potential as a positive influence, especially for young people. Her suggestion is to give youth, who watch a lot of television, the chance to make television more relevant to their lives. Guinness and her full-time staff of 10 start from the premise that most television for the 13-to-18-year-old market fails teenagers by patronising them.

Asked how one successfully combines multicultural and multiethnic teens, some confused, others downright rebellious, with expensive television equipment and rigorous production schedules, Guinness says, "We concentrate on giving them a sense of ownership, and usually an attitude of responsibility follows."

The sense of ownership is not an illusion. The young people fill all production roles from grip to director to 'talent'. They produce their own shows from their scripts in what comes to feel very much like their studio. They are responsible for all aspects of the production; Guinness and her staff are principally advisers.

For youths who have a tough time picturing what they will be doing next week, let alone five years from now, YCTV offers short-term goals – skills – and long-term goals – jobs.

Luke Hyams, 19, hosted the Jagger interview. A handsome young man with an open, friendly, conversational style, Hyams may be on his way to a television career thanks to YCTV. Four years ago, his life was on a much different track.

"I had a difficult time at a school in London which eventually asked me to leave. No other school wanted to take me in. I had no job qualifications, no future."

Things started to get better when he heard about YCTV. "I was able to dive straight into a new kind of education where I learned lots of different 'televisual' skills."

Hyams has been involved with many cable productions in his nearly five years at YCTV, but *Pass the Mike* is a show he has guided since just after the basic concept was created. It was the first show the organisation sold to a broadcast, rather than cable, station.

Hyams realises what a great opportunity he has been given. "I have interviewed some amazing people. Besides Mick Jagger, there have been Tony Blair, Prince Nazeem and many others."

Of the more than 800 kids associated with YCTV over the last six years, most, like Hyams, learned about it through the grapevine or a family friend.

Voodoo
listens to the
[corporate]
fool

Being in YCTV is more like a job than being a student, and participants in the programme are officially termed 'members'. YCTV is similar to a professional television production company, but one at which profits are plowed back into a foundation.

Some other shows in production are *Cinemania,* movie news and reviews, and *Underground Soundz,* a music show previewing up-and-coming bands from a teen perspective.

The foundation believes its mission is to give these young people social, communication and problem-solving skills they can use in the real world. In the context of television production, they learn practical uses for once-boring subjects like mathematics (for budgets), writing (scripts) and how to use both print and electronic sources for research.

Each year's budget is a challenge, as is it for most nonprofit organisations, but Guinness also has a dream of expanding to 'sister studios' in Los Angeles and New York. "With proper funding, we would be ready to set up a YCTV-USA studio. We are applying for the necessary tax status in the U.S. and hope to start the ball rolling in the fall."

When the audience had been waiting for 45 minutes to see Jagger and Hyams finally took his seat on-stage, some of the edge was off the anticipation. The buzz in the gallery was that Jagger had arrived in the building but that his studio entrance was delayed by a technical glitch. But teenage host Hyams appeared cool and calm.

Jagger arrived. Hyams questioned. Jagger answered. And soon another show was wrapped.

All in all, just another day at work for the production staff at YCTV.

... "This is Steve Tice, for Business News, Notting Hill, London."

Notes on notepad found by the chambermaid next to your bed:

SABRINA GUINNESS

- ◆ Built YCTV
- ◆ Captured talent (multicultural)
- ◆ Interesting background, It girl, Prince Charles' girlfriend, Guinness heiress
- ◆ Identified you need money to make it in the movie biz – not talent
- ◆ No money, no chance
- ◆ Went to LA
- ◆ Worked in projects providing opportunities for local people with talent to shine through – e.g. Spike Lee
- ◆ Had a vision to bring it to London

- ◆ Employed recently retired people from the BBC
- ◆ *Pass the Mike* idea of talented 14/15 year old (Peter Mandelson – Tony Blair) – now on BBC mainstream TV
- ◆ Contacts, Harrison Ford, Dan Ackroyd, Greg Dyke (Chairman), Mick J.

Maybe you get what you ask for if you've got the chutzpah?

- ◆ In what ways can our company search for talent where we wouldn't normally look?
- ◆ How can we bridge the digital divide in Ourco – youth + experience?

Article in inflight magazine, in between an article on how not to offend other cultures over a business lunch, and one on high-tech surveillance measures

E stands for E-Education

Fulfilling their UK election pledge, Tony Blair and David Blunkett have moved education, education, education to the top of their policy agenda. This is right, and it has huge implications for the nation. But it also has a serious and so far underestimated impact on another of the government's main ambitions, to make the UK the European centre and driving force for e-business. Blair's famous and praiseworthy support for 'joined-up government' should lead him to understand that our national interests in education and in a thriving e-business sector are in fact inextricably linked. Our kids need to be educated to play their part in the e-world. And a vibrant and expanding e-business must be there to employ them when they're ready.

New Labour has enunciated a simple but compelling vision for education in the twenty-first century. The stated purpose is to ensure that every child achieves as well as he or she can. Note 'every'. As long as one child underperforms, the mission statement is unfulfilled. Starting with the basics, the focus so far has been on standards of literacy and numeracy and on social exclusion, providing more for the pupils at the bottom of the ladder of opportunity.

Voodoo lives beyond the curriculum

This is a balancing act. Education must be about revealing to children the joy of learning, as well as equipping them for future employment. But to critics who complain that the new syllabus is too humdrum and too vocational, the government can convincingly respond that learning opportunities are not great for those who can neither read nor count, nor for those who find themselves trapped in hopeless social contexts, like the kids on some run-down London estates.

Nobody doubts that there is a pressing need for education and training to fill the oft-mentioned skills gap. There is a limit to how many skilled professionals the UK can import from other countries without playing beggar my neighbour. But when the needs of all and sundry are assessed – the nation, business, public services, government itself – one set of players is often taken for granted or totally ignored. Teachers.

Voodoo loves maths; voodoo loves dance

Teachers and educationalists have been engulfed in the last 20 years by an avalanche of change. They have been given little chance to adapt to one wave before the next has broken over their heads. All these changes have been well meant. But who ever stopped to ask, when a new set of tests and assessments was introduced, how teachers were to make time for them in a day already bursting at the seams? It's important that this point be made by people like us who are neither teachers nor union officials. Yet today teachers are faced by another problem, just as awkward as all the others. They are trying to guide pupils through a maze which the kids know better than they do.

Voodoo asks: in what way would the company have to change for your value to be maximised?

We mean, of course, the IT maze. A large and explosively growing percentage of kids now come from homes that make them more IT-literate and more internet-aware than their teachers. If their homes don't have kit, probably their friends' homes do. In the UK, schools spend on average 4% of their budgets on IT. With desperate shortages of funds for books and building maintenance, you can't really blame them. Here are some facts. There are 500,000 teachers employed in state education. There are 25,000 unfilled vacancies. The average age of Britain's teachers is – are you sitting down? – nearly 50! Most people of that age are not naturally at home in the IT world. How could they be? So their pupils come to school with a deeper and wider experience in IT than their teachers. But here's the rub. That experience is haphazardly gathered. The kids have no structured or managed approach to the growth of their capabilities, and are unlikely to gain it at school.

Voodoo loves immediacy

The cultural problem is deep. Traditional education has always been founded on the accretion of knowledge over years. The pupils now demand immediacy. They want to see the immediate usefulness of what they learn. Traditional education also favoured the acquisition of knowledge. IT poses in its most acute form the question whether knowing something is necessarily better than knowing how to find it out. Should pupils spend ages learning the dates of the kings and queens of England, or just the URL of a decent encyclopaedia? Should they learn how to calculate cos and sin, or how to use a calculator? Can they better use their time in the classroom gaining skills rather than specific knowledge?

Voodoo lives and works in the neighbourhood

There's a role for industry here, too. The magazine publisher IPC Magazines had over 3000 PCs in their office. Through their Corporate Citizenship programme, they mentored some local schools, shipping out to them hardware which, no longer suitable for the company's state-of-the-art needs, was still perfectly usable – and much better than anything the school budget would run to. IPC also shipped out expertise and guidance on how to integrate and use the kit. They helped the teachers as well as the kids. It was a real joy to meet teachers who realised that just for once someone was trying to do something *for* them and not *to* them. Maybe your business will be linked to an education net.

You seach for a relatively blank page in the inflight magazine – there's one here for a watch, big Gulliver wrist on white tablecloth that will do fine – and jot down the following:

We have no doubt that if we looked at our society as it is today – multicultural, fast, competitive, digital – and started designing an education system to suit, it would look very different from what we have now.

We are facing an unacknowledged crisis. Teaching used to be a family tradition. Nowadays few teachers would encourage their children to follow in their footsteps. They feel themselves to be underpaid, undervalued, berated by all and sundry, from Ofsted to the parents of their pupils, seeing far too big a slice of the total education budget in the sticky fingers of town and county halls. It's not so long ago that a British government derecognised the teaching unions, a deliberate insult from which the profession has not yet fully recovered. Would they have dared do the same thing to doctors or nurses?

Can IT help? We believe it can. IT may not be the best solution to the education crisis we are facing. But it may be the only one. Here's our vision of the school of the future. A limited number of large schools in a region have the best teachers and the best technology. They are of course networked to share resources. But dozens of other schools (not necessarily all geographically close) are networked too, sharing text, data, voice and video. In these schools trained assistants who know how to get the best for their pupils from the shared resource shoulder much of the teaching load. The schools form a huge interactive community, developing skills, knowledge, even wisdom across the web.

HOW ARE WE EDUCATING PEOPLE?

Education System
◆ At meltdown
◆ Average age of teachers 50+
◆ Never grew up with computers
◆ Kids want interaction
◆ They are our future
◆ Fast world
◆ Tony Blair said 'UK Plc Centre of e-business for the World'
◆ Yet teachers – depressed and suppressed section of society
◆ Job descriptions changed annually by well-meaning governments
◆ National Curriculum changed annually by well-meaning governments
◆ Measurements of success changed annually by well-meaning governments
◆ Teachers used to come from teaching dynasties – not now
◆ Methods of teaching have been exploded by the internet
◆ In the internet world we need facilitators not teachers
◆ Must stop thinking academia is the only path to talent

and then

◆ how similar is the educational background of the last 20 people we hired?

and then

◆ do something

Back at the office, after a call from you on the plane's seatback phone – your first time – your PA finds, from amongst all the pile of crap on your desk, the report **All Our Futures: Creativity, Culture and Education:** *a major report on the future of education by the National Advisory Committee on Creative and Cultural Education (NACCCE).*

And she types up the following sections which you highlighted with a yellow marker pen earlier that week:

The Government has repeatedly emphasised that education is its top priority. The major task, it has said, must be to help all young people to keep pace with, and contribute to, a world of rapid economic and cultural change. In this respect, the Prime Minister has emphasised the vital need to develop the creative abilities of all young people. The NACCCE strongly endorsed these objectives. We also found deep concerns throughout education that many of the existing pressures on schools militate against achieving them.

Education worldwide faces unprecedented challenges: economic, technological, social, and personal. Policymakers stress the urgent need to develop 'human resources' – in particular, creativity, adaptability, and better powers of communication. *All Our Futures* argues that this means reviewing some of the most basic assumptions about education. It means new approaches and priorities based on broader concepts of young people's abilities, of how to motivate them and promote their self-esteem, and of developing the skills and aptitudes they require – and this means a much stronger emphasis on creative and cultural education.

Voodoo works on all levels at once: the voodoo is in the system

The economic challenge is to develop in young people the skills, knowledge and personal qualities they need for a world where work is undergoing rapid and long-term change.

The technological challenge is to enable young people to make their way with confidence in a world that is being shaped by technologies which are evolving more quickly than at any time in history.

The social challenge is to provide forms of education that enable young people to engage positively and confidently with far-reaching processes of social and cultural change.

The personal challenge is to develop the unique capacities of all young people, and to provide a basis on which they can build lives that are purposeful and fulfilling.

Voodoo looks beyond the first impression

There are many misconceptions about creativity. Some people associate it only with the arts, or particular types of individual, or think it cannot be 'taught' or nurtured. Our concept of creativity recognises the potential for creative achievement in all fields of human activity; and the capacity for such achievements in the many and not the few. Creativity is not a single power but multidimensional. Creative ability develops through practical application, and this involves using techniques and skills in the discipline in question, and some general features of creative processes that apply across all disciplines. Creative processes involve using imagination, pursuing purposes, being original and judging value.

We define creativity as: imaginative activity fashioned so as to produce outcomes that are both original and of value.

Voodoo experiments in order to create

Two dynamics drive these creative processes:

◆ **Freedom and control:** Creative processes require both the freedom to experiment and the use of skills, knowledge and understanding.

◆ **Creativity and culture:** Creative development is intimately related to cultural development. Creativity is not a wholly individual process. Creative achievement often draws from the ideas and achievements of others. Just as different modes of thinking interact in a single mind, individual creativity is affected by dialogue with others.

Voodoo connects in order to create

Creativity is a basic capacity of human intelligence. Our ability to represent experience in various ways is fundamental to how we think and communicate. Words help us to formulate some ideas but not others. We think about the world in the many ways we experience it: visually, in sound, in movement, and so on. Conventional education tends to emphasise academic ability and, in particular, verbal and mathematical reasoning. These are vital to young people's intellectual development, but they are not the whole of intelligence.

Voodoo says: important but not sufficient

This multifaceted nature of intelligence has two important implications for education, and for creative education in particular. First, it is neither accurate nor responsible to judge children's intelligence on the basis of academic abilities alone. All children have a profile of abilities across a wide range of intelligences. Second, children who perform poorly in conventional academic tests may have strong abilities in other areas. Judging children against a single standard of ability can misrepresent their own individual strengths.

Voodoo accelerates education and wealth

Voodoo distrusts old measures

In future, education will be much more a shared enterprise. It will be continuous and open-ended, and provided by schools and colleges, by businesses and commercial organisations, by new technologies, by artists, scientists, other professionals, and by the community at large. The Government has a pivotal role in creating a vision for education and setting a course. Many of our proposals are therefore addressed directly to the Government. But just as education should be a collaborative enterprise, many others must lend their resources and expertise.

Voodoo takes a stand

Home.

As you put your travel case down in the hallway, your daughter runs in to embrace you.

You smell her hair on your face, lift her from the floor. Hug her tightly.

Later, over dinner, she hands you a letter from school.

DEAR PARENT...

As part of our Community Outreach programme, I'm attaching a small booklet called *You Can Make a Difference for Kids*. We are sending this to parents who – like you – have prominent positions in the business community. Our intention is to seek your advice on our forming similar sorts of collaborative ventures with the business world to the one that is represented by this booklet. Why? So that we too can make a difference in our pupils' lives, outside the formal structure of the curriculum.

You Can Make a Difference for Kids was developed as a collaboration between the American Search Institute and the technology and innovation company 3M, as part of the latter's commitment to its employees and customers, their families, their communities and the employees of the future.

(The Search Institute is an independent, nonprofit, nonsectarian organisation whose mission is to advance the well-being of adolescents and children by generating knowledge and promoting its application.)

The booklet sums up a behavioural approach for increasing the confidence and creativity of young people by providing them with what are known as External and Internal Assets.

The first 20 developmental assets focus on positive experiences that young people receive from the people and institutions in their lives. Four categories of external assets are included in the framework:

External assets:
Support

Young people need to experience support, care, and love from their families, neighbours, and many others. They need organisations and institutions that provide positive, supportive environments.

Empowerment

Young people need to be valued by their community and have opportunities to contribute to others. For this to occur, they must be safe and feel secure.

Boundaries and expectations

Young people need to know what is expected of them and whether activities and behaviours are 'in bounds' and 'out of bounds'.

Constructive use of time

Young people need constructive, enriching opportunities for growth through creative activities, youth programmes, congregational involvement, and quality time at home.

Internal assets:

A community's responsibility for its young does not end with the provision of external assets. There needs to be a similar commitment to nurturing the internal qualities that guide choices and create a sense of centredness, purpose and focus. Indeed, shaping internal dispositions that encourage wise, responsible and compassionate judgements is particularly important in a society that prizes individualism. Four categories of internal assets are included in the framework:

Commitment to learning

Young people need to develop a lifelong commitment to education and learning.

Positive values

Young people need to develop strong values that guide their choices.

Social competencies

Young people need skills and competencies that equip them to make positive choices, to build relationships, and to succeed in life.

Positive identity

Young people need a strong sense of their own power, purpose, worth and promise.

We hope that you will review this booklet and give us your feedback on both its content and its intentions.

Perhaps I could call you to solicit your advice on our school forming similar positive, constructive relationships between the worlds of education and business?

Yours faithfully,
J Tredegar (Ms)
Head of Lower School

You type 3M into google.com and are taken straight to their website.

| About 3M | Investor Relations | Our Environment | Results | Sales $15 billion | History | Corporate Culture |

You double click

McKNIGHT PRINCIPLES

William L. McKnight Management Principles
Created 3M's Corporate Culture

William L. McKnight joined Minnesota Mining and Manufacturing Company in 1907 as an assistant bookkeeper. He quickly rose through the company, becoming president in 1929 and chairman of the board in 1949.

Many believe McKnight's greatest contribution was as a business philosopher, since he created a corporate culture that encourages employee initiative, innovation and provides secure employment.

His basic rule of management was laid out in 1948:
"As our business grows, it becomes increasingly necessary to delegate responsibility and to encourage men and women to exercise their initiative. This requires considerable tolerance. Those men and women to whom we delegate authority and responsibility, if they are good people, are going to want to do their jobs in their own way.

"Mistakes will be made. But if a person is essentially right, the mistakes he or she makes are not as serious in the long run as the mistakes management will make if it undertakes to tell those in authority exactly how they must do their jobs."

"Management that is destructively critical when mistakes are made kills initiative. And it's essential that we have many people with initiative if we are to continue to grow."

Voodoo asks: in what ways should you be fearful of yourself?

Your eyes return to the top of the page. His basic rule of management was laid out in 1948.

And you think: And what are we doing in terms of initiative and risk taking, and honouring our people, 50-odd years later?

Voodoo embraces everything...

You open the gift-wrapped book from Amazon: Essays For Tomorrow.
Who sent you this? No note.

Voodoo likes a nice surprise

You open the book at the following page:

Re-inventing diversity: the internet – the world's tool?

What's one tough lesson that I've learned about doing business on the Internet? It's important to have a diverse team. I'm not talking about just gender or race. I mean diversity of skills and temperament. It's hard to get your team composition right. At the beginning, you need more diversity than you can imagine. When we started iVillage, we didn't have enough technical people or really anal analytical people. Instead, we had a surplus of people who could sell our story to customers and advertisers – which is great. But you still need people to build the subways. That lack of diversity slowed us down in the beginning.

But as critical as diversity is at the beginning, once you start to scale, you want the opposite: a team of minds that think alike. Otherwise, you get gridlock. As iVillage grew, creative gridlock threatened our team's cohesiveness. I had to deal with intuitive people, analytical people, lyrical people, and worrywarts. It took a lot of work to get everyone to trust one another.

Candice Carpenter Co-founder and chairman iVillage Inc New York, New York, Fast Company
February 2001

The connected e-world of the twenty-first century presents us all with an unprecedented opportunity.

Such a sentence, such an opening to an article is usually a preface to a description of some groundbreaking technology, or an uncannily comprehensive methodology. In other words, the twenty-first century has begun in the same pornographic flush of excitement as we ended the twentieth, and 'unprecedented opportunity' means one thing: money. How much and how quickly can we all make some e-money? Just a couple of years ago, the big question used to be: 'Does anyone know anyone who is making money from the web?' Remember? Now the question is: 'How can we catch up with those who appear to be on the point of making unimaginable sums of money on the web?' Or 'How can we avoid becoming the next company to blow a huge amount of venture capital investment on champagne and First Class transatlantic flights?'

But what if there was something else to the internet beyond money? What if this conjunction of technical possibility with human imagination and ingenuity was happening for some other reason than simply to give us all alternative routes of trade and sources of revenue? Consider that the new currency, the new metric of success is not money, but relationship.

What if we were being asked to face up to our relationships with others – no matter where on the planet they were, no matter what their background or conditioning? That means facing up in a fresh way to an old business issue: diversity.

The web is a symbol and manifestation of human diversity, a product of individual and collective self-expression, free of the constraints of censure, censorship or prejudice. That's maybe why some people are so scared or intolerant of it.

Voodoo warns: who you are is your future

Voodoo hates blandness

René Carayol, net entrepreneur and commentator, looks beyond the internet as a new economic model:

"I see the web as an opportunity for the business world to embrace basic human values such as equity and fairness. I see a way to by-pass the often clumsy attempts by which organisations have attempted to 'manage diversity' in such formal schemes as Equal Opportunities and positive discrimination. Now we can value individuals as much as social groups.

"The Internet has no 'isms'. Anybody who has access can communicate and compete today. The web has no geographical barriers. We're used to making that point nowadays so it's become a bit blasé, but it's truly earth-shattering for a world constructed around physical and political space. The death of distance may also be the death of barriers. On the internet nobody knows whether you are black, white, male, female, gay, straight – we have the opportunity to build the secular society, we have the opportunity to involve everyone. How many times have I wanted to buy goods from South Africa, the United States, Australia and had to wait for a holiday? Now I can surf the net and someone in, say, Botswana can connect with me. That's good for me, of course, but it's also amazing for them. Everybody has the opportunity today to communicate; everybody has the opportunity to be someone.

"Take the Gambia where my mother lives: ISPs and internet cafés are replacing the archaic phone system. In a country where the post is definitely snail mail and some houses don't even have addresses, the internet has exploded. All over the West Coast of Africa people are communicating with each other in this way. It's fantastic.

"In the past managing diversity has meant 'how do we create a diverse society that has more equal access to education?' The internet has upped the stakes. As a boy growing up in London, I belonged to a football team and we went on a trip to France. Three-quarters of our team had never left London. Now those boys leave via the internet. They travel the Global Village via the internet. I had a pen friend in South Yarra and it took three weeks to exchange letters; my 10-year-old daughter has 'click friends' all over the world and the exchange is instant. Her 'click friends' could be black, white, male, female, young, old – who knows? It doesn't matter. By being able to communicate in a way that makes those distinctions irrelevant, they are allowed to do what we are all trying to do: connect with those who share a common interest.

"Yes, there's the money, and the need for money. One could say building and delivering an internet business is the largest and most significant legal wealth creation mechanism the world has ever seen. One of the major drivers behind the internet is focusing on the time-poor, money - rich community, so the internet trades in instant gratification. But the wealth creation is a means and not the end. This is absolutely the most exciting time to be in the technology industry. And all of a sudden we are not just delivering technology, we are changing lives. We are transforming businesses. We are breaking down barriers. How important does that make us?

"I will encourage my children to have friends from all over the world, breaking down cultural barriers, age barriers. Common interest is no longer religious, no longer geographical, no longer about what social grouping you belong to. It's about what passion and ideas you can share with other human beings."

Voodoo embraces the new rules of attraction

Voodoo connects to a powerful future

Passion and ideas drive the new breed of fast businesses. Certainly the e-business world has generated new rules of engagement, which are themselves created, not so much by introducing something new, as by dismantling the barriers to open and clear relationships, the barriers which inhibit talent. Evidently we have thrown away the necessity to have 20 years of business experience before you become a director of your business. The focus now is on your imagination and courage as much as your expertise. Old Slow business used to actively discourage diversity. Becoming a director meant setting out on a long, long journey whose aim was to prove that you were 'one of us'. If you were seen to be sufficiently 'like us' in mind-set, values, behaviour and dress code, you'd get the job – eventually. But Fast business is inclusive of everyone.

Spend time with any internet start-up and you'll see how passion and imagination are the drivers behind the astonishing creativity apparent in the e-world today. Perhaps that urge is more attractive to our sense of being human than that of money making. It's also true that creativity is the building blocks of the new wealth. And creativity demands diversity of thinking and perspective: it cannot exist without it. (No one on the web became a billionaire by conforming.)

Kalinka Poullain is co-founder of Yesindeed.com and now working on the launch of Generic Intelligence. Her experience is that diversity is an opportunity and not a barrier:

"Everything is amazingly fast on the net", she says. "Whether it be the evolution of the technology, services, or acquisition of customers. To keep up with that speed of evolution you have to think very fast and big and multidimensionally. The brain seems to love that kind of challenge and everybody I know who works on new products (whatever they are) on that market seem to have an increase in creativity. It's as if the mind expands when it is thinking and working in that kind of frame. People working in this industry seem to have changed their time perception (one day for me feels almost like a week). But after a while you get used to it."

At the same time, learning and knowledge sharing works so much faster than in normal industries, not just because of the speed of contact, but because of its immediacy.

"You can see what others do on the same field and go further. The learning ladder is so much steeper. You can talk easily to anybody through e-mail. You want to contact that writer (perhaps you loved his book), a few clicks and here and there and you are talking directly to someone who could be anywhere in the world. It's a bit like the cosmonauts when they looked at Planet Earth from up there: you see one planet, but you don't see any frontier. The internet gives that feeling too."

But there is still more, in Kalinka's experience:

"The internet and its inherent capability for sorting, cross-referencing and transmitting information across the planet at the speed of light, is the technology that makes people's visions something more than an impossible dream. The internet offers an exciting new paradigm – a paradigm of self-managed care in which individuals have the knowledge and the power to control their personal and collective evolution. We are heading to what we could call 'Conscious Evolution'."

So what can we do tomorrow in our own companies to embrace some of this 'new diversity'?

Voodoo believes differences are creative

René Carayol again: "Without a doubt the first and foremost most important thing is to stop recruiting skills. How many times have we heard 'you hired me for my skills and fired me for my personality'? Let's start hiring personalities, no matter what the skills. Let's focus on contents not packaging. Or if you are thinking packaging, use it consciously, use it as part of the business strategy. Look at the two key players in lastminute.com, Brent Hoberman and Martha Lane Fox, and how they were PR'd so effectively in the press prior to their market launch. This is to do with appropriate roles. Nothing to do with gender, it's to do with eloquence, artistic talent and enthusiasm. He is the socially inept backroom boy, but quite possibly the brains of the outfit. She in the new economy is the appropriate spokesperson and living embodiment of the brand – young, attractive, successful, a woman, very media friendly. In the new business world, appearance and packaging is all about 'fit to purpose'. In the old business world Martha Lane Fox would be simply decoration.

"But generally, I think male/female, black/white, Jewish/Catholic are increasingly sterile debates. What I ask as I look at a list of candidates for any new position in the companies I work for is: 'who has the social mix I am looking for?' They are the winners for my organisation but of course that mix will be different for every company.

"When I look at the Board of Directors at IPC Electric we have had Spanish, South African, Australian, Irish, Black, Female, Gay. And our HQ was London. From one point of view you are able to say that it doesn't matter a jot where they are from. But from another point of view, you're able to point out that it is that eclectic mix of styles and backgrounds that makes it such a brilliant team.

"That's a contrast to my previous position as IT Director of IPC (the non-Electric). When I went for my interview with Mike Matthew CEO, I asked his PA, who was black, how many black managers there were at IPC. The answer was 'none'. I asked "Does this make it a good place for me to come and work?" "Yes," she replied, "you can help make the difference." Now, I never believe in overt campaigning or positive discrimination. There's nothing worse than the wrong person in the wrong position, no matter what colour. There are too many examples of great positions and poor incumbents, who may have satisfied some quota system, but have served only to disappoint, and perhaps close the door to any further person of colour. However, my guess is that if you do a good enough job, it encourages your peers to look for talent in places they've never looked before. Not everyone needs to be Anglo-Saxon, middle class and male. When I joined IPC there were no black senior managers, when I left there were a number of highly respected non-white senior managers. This was achieved not by campaigning but by allowing people to be the best they could be.

"Again we have the theme of getting out of the way to allow people to express their innate talents, rather than prove their compliance to a corporate or cultural norm. This leads us each to the demands of taking self-responsibility, not just for our careers, but for how we see the world. Geraldine Bown of Domino Consulting Ltd (www.dominoconsultancy.co.uk) has for 14 years been helping organisations implement diversity programmes (just one of her many clients has been Hewlett Packard). She has seen a shift from an emphasis on compliance and legal implications to one which encourages each individual to take responsibility for their own value system, prejudice and attitudes."

"Much training has been about adopting a code of behaviour towards others – not about increasing the individual's awareness of their own value system and how they acquired it. The critical need now is to impact how people are 'being' as opposed to how they are 'doing'."

The barriers to diversity, then, exist in our heads long before they show up in our actions. And the start point for change is in us in a more real and urgent way than it ever could be in a set of guidelines or quotas.

"We **don't** try to get our participants to change their attitudes, but we do challenge them to move out of their comfort zones and see that if they are uncomfortable with someone it is probably more to do with themselves than it is to do with the person they are uncomfortable with. In this way we can get real about our own projections.

"Our heads tell us that we would never allow our personal opinions to affect our professional judgements – in fact we all do it it a lot of the time, and we are able to show people just how this happens. We have to stop pretending prejudice doesn't happen – or resolving that we won't do it – and be realistic about taking responsibility for who we are and how we react to others and why. If we have a problem with someone – based on an aspect of their difference as opposed to inappropriate unacceptable behaviour – then we have to be prepared to look at *ourselves* first and deal honestly with our own issues. This is 'heart' work and is extremely powerful."

So, having ignored for a few pages of this magazine the economic potential of the internet, it is worth concluding by reminding ourselves of the bottom-line business benefit of diversity. Having a diverse workforce and managing it properly is a competitive strategy that can help attract diverse customers. In a global enterprise that is a critical competence. And diversity also benefits the internal corporate culture, in at least two ways.

Voodoo gets together

Firstly, organisations are social creations, which by their nature acknowledge and value their members, if only because they **are** members. Widen the membership, and you increase the organisation's capacity to be a symbol of its acknowledgement and support of people. And in this business climate, where competition for 'the best talent' is one of the major obsessions, we need to look at all ways in which we can make ourselves into greater valuers of human beings.

Secondly, organisations are intellectual products – a result of how we agree to think. If we all think the same, because we have come from the same background or because we have conditioned ourselves to copy each other to ensure recognition and progression, we reduce our ability to stretch our intellectual resource. Unchallenged, our thinking calcifies, thus increasing our organisational tendency to go deaf and blind to a changing world.

If we can recruit employees who have different perspectives, we can embrace those differences to act as a catalyst for the creativity of the organisation. When the imperative is to generate ideas and solutions quicker than the competition, being surrounded by 'yes men' could be tantamount to business suicide.

Robert Lattimer, a leading authority on the subject of 'diversity thinking', has found that homogeneous groups may reach consensus more quickly but will not generate as many new ideas or solve problems as well as diverse groups.

Voodoo is bored by sameness

Voodoo says: consensus is no way to run a company

An article from Fortune Magazine about Ernest H Drew, CEO of Hoechst Celanese, the chemical giant, supports his theory:

He was attending a conference for Hoechst's top 125 officers, mostly white men, who were joined by 50 or so lower level women and minorities. The group split into problem-solving teams, some mixed by race and sex, others all white and male. The main issue was how the corporate culture affected the business and what changes might be made to improve results. When the teams presented their findings, a light clicked on for Drew. 'It was so obvious that the diverse teams had the broader solutions', he recalls. 'They had ideas I hadn't even thought of. For the first time we realised that diversity is a strength as it relates to problem solving. Before we just thought of diversity as the total number of minorities and women in the company, like affirmative action. Now we knew we needed diversity at every level of the company where decisions are made'.

"Men", said Confucius in the days before our first attempts at Managing Diversity spawned Politically Correct Language, "draw together by their very nature, but habits and customs keep them apart".

Perhaps the web, creation and symbol of humanity's innate diversity, will teach us all to let go of at least some of those old habits and customs.

On the inside front cover, you write:

TEN QUESTIONS I CAN ASK MY TEAM TO ENCOURAGE DIVERSITY THINKING

◆ Who do you know?

◆ Who's different in your team?

◆ Why?

◆ What's the balance like?

◆ What don't we know?

◆ What wouldn't we like to know?

◆ Where do we look for 'talent'?

◆ What do you want to destroy?

◆ Who can help?

◆ What's the right balance between 'embracing diversity' and 'a common corporate culture'?

And then:

DIVERSITY MESSAGES

◆ Internet.in Africa – big new phenomenon

◆ No names on roads or numbers on doors

◆ Hopeless phone system – but –

◆ Queues for 15 minutes for internet cafés

◆ Advent of digital/satellite TV/internet mobiles – connect people to the world

◆ Global village

◆ Kids now want the latest trainers/Man Utd shirts

◆ Dangerous Americana commercialism – high crime (they missed the industrialisation)

◆ But MacDonalds or Pizza Hut in Africa?

◆ Substandard goods – best they can get

◆ Increasingly exclusive world

◆ How can we justify multiethnic multicultural Europe dumping on country of origin?

And

What should our company BE to operate more effectively in this world?

Notes (found by your partner) jotted in the margins of the back page of morning newspaper.

SPORT

- Football managers – is there a new breed coming in?
- Old School, George Graham, Alex Ferguson, David O'Leary: command control like headmaster at school, suits and ties
- New Wave: Gianluca Vialli, Arsene Wenger etc., always talk up players' *esprit de corps,* discuss, share, track suits

Diversity thinking in sports

- England Cricket – Duncan Fletcher from Zimbabwe
- Wales Rugby Union – a New Zealand coach Graham Henry (heard he has a website)
- Redgrave, Pinsent the rowers – foreign coach
- Boxers – foreign trainers
- Greg Rusedski – foreign coach

The outcasting of Clinton Morrison – experience over talent – the British way!

And you think: How does talent show up?

Where it forces itself? Where you look for it? Where you give it licence? (YCTV)

Where you embrace it, rather than direct it.

Where do leaders show up?

Not from academia. Not from the board of directors. It shows up where passion is. Where truth speaks.

After the Stephen Lawrence murder:
Neville Lawrence – now a leader of the Black Community

After the Damilola Taylor murder:
Richard Taylor speaks out – "the family value has been bastardised and allowed to go to the dogs"
– Positive leaders. But not educated

E-MAIL 52 later that morning in the office

From: Jill Thorn
Subject: Mentoring
Date: Fri, 16 Feb 2001 10:22:59 –0000
MIME-Version: 1.0
X-Priority: 3 (Normal)
Importance: Normal
X-Loop-Detect: 1

Hi there again.

You wanted some information about the Mentoring Scheme at IPC – here goes. So you're thinking of bringing it in at your place eh? Great. I hope you get out of it what we have.

OK Here goes.

The Mentoring Scheme at IPC has been running for around 5 years now and it is in conjunction with the Roots and Wings Scheme. We currently mentor students from Deptford Green and John Roan Schools.

The Roots and Wings Scheme has been running for around 8 years now and they have just applied for Charitable Status but have relied on private and public funding in the past.

PwC, SG Warburg and Citibank are amongst other companies involved in this scheme.

Basically this is how the scheme works:
◆ A mentoring assembly is held at the school by the scheme co-ordinators, looking for pupils who are interested. Kids from all abilities are chosen in the age range 13-15; there are some who are really failing at school, some are having a hard time at home (most of them come from deprived areas/families), some are high achievers who don't have any social life, some have achieved well in the past but have started to slip into bad ways.

◆ We currently have around 35 mentors at IPC – some have been mentors for a few years and the new group which I recruited have been going since September.

◆ Some relationships don't work out whilst some mentees become personal friends of the mentors and their families.

◆ We usually find that there is something definite that a mentor can offer a mentee e.g. one boy wants to join the army and his mentor is an ex-navy officer, one girl is an avid Arsenal supporter and her mentor works on a football title.

◆ Once the matching has been arranged we organise a trip for the mentors to go and meet their mentees at the school (and they stay for school dinners – a really fun day!).

◆ Then we arrange two organised visits for the pupils to come to IPC – some of them have never even been up to London so it's quite an event for them.

◆ What the mentees get out of it is improved confidence, ambition, broader horizons; they get to spend time in an office environment and they have someone who isn't a teacher or a parent to discuss any issues with.

◆ The mentors also get a lot out of helping these kids and seeing the difference it makes to them – the atmosphere on the coach coming back from the trip to the school is something I never experience with the same people in the office!

◆ The scheme has to prove that they are making a difference in order to get funding so every year they do proper research into the difference it is making to the pupils and it is proven that those on the scheme definitely do better academically but also their personal skills improve too.

Hope this helps, any other info needed then please give me a call.

Regards,
Jill Thorn

You feel that something has begun to move.

Why shouldn't business be a positive influence on the development of a country's future, through taking an active role in the growth of people – rather than seeing them purely as tools, units, resources in its economy?

From now on you'll make sure that this organisation embraces the future by embracing information and influence from all sources. Live the movie. Open up, act with courage, connect with the customer, concentrate on the core, build alliances...

Excellent.

Now, what next?

Forwarded from a friend.

Junk mail. You are about to hit the delete button, when the first line catches your eye.

E-MAIL 53

If we could shrink the earth's population to a village of precisely 100 people, with all the existing human ratios remaining the same, it would look something like the following:

There would be:

57 Asians

21 Europeans

14 from the Western Hemisphere, both north and south

8 Africans

52 would be female

48 would be male

70 would be non-white

30 would be white

70 would be non-Christian

30 would be Christian

89 would be heterosexual

11 would be homosexual

6 people would possess 59% of the entire world's wealth and all 6 would be from the United States.

80 would live in substandard housing

70 would be unable to read

50 would suffer from malnutrition

1 would be near death; 1 would be near birth

1 would have a college education

1 would own a computer

When one considers our world from such a compressed perspective, the need for acceptance, understanding and education becomes glaringly apparent.

The following is also something to ponder ...

Voodoo says choose, then choose again.

If you woke up this morning with more health than illness ... you are more blessed than the million who will not survive this week.

If you have never experienced the danger of battle, the loneliness of imprisonment, the agony of torture, or the pangs of starvation ... you are ahead of 500 million people in the world.

If you can attend a church meeting without fear of harassment, arrest, torture or death ... you are more blessed than 3 billion people in the world.

If you have food in the refrigerator, clothes on your back, a roof overhead and a place to sleep ... you are richer than 75% of this world.

If you have money in the bank, in your wallet, and spare change in a dish someplace ... you are among the top 8% of the world's wealthy.

If your parents are still alive and still married ... you are very rare, even in the United States and Canada.

If you can read this message, you just received a double blessing in that someone was thinking of you, and furthermore, you are more blessed than over 2 billion people in the world who cannot read at all.

Someone once said: What goes around comes around.

Work like you don't need the money.

Love like you've never been hurt.

Dance like nobody's watching.

Sing like nobody's listening.

Live like it's Heaven on Earth.

You select 'Forward to' from the drop-down folder and select 10 people from your address book, click, click, click...

Voodoo is not afraid...

From the pre-conference reading pack

Dear Delegate,

Welcome to our Third International Conference on Strategy and Innovation. Our theme this year is *Blueprints for Future Success* and we have a range of speakers who we believe will give you compelling insights into where your organisation needs to be focusing its efforts over the coming months.

We hope the following extracts from recent press articles give some interesting context for this conference.

Enjoy!

Yours faithfully,
The Conference Organisers and Sponsors

Success? Think people, take risks

Extract from article about **Daniel Gestetner**,
CEO Shopsmart.com
The Times January 18, 2001

The average age of Shopsmart's workforce is 27, so like any other dot.com CEO he has had to combine astute dealmaking with emnotional intelligence and leadership skills. "It seems to work – only a handful of people have left in two years. I was looking for smart people who were not afraid to take a risk and who don't like structured environments. People who would get behind what we were doing. Successful businesses bring people in and empower them. So we say, if you have an idea, tell us. A lot of multinationals have lost sight of the fact that it's the people who got them where they are..."

Question and response in same article:
Q: Where will you be in 20 years' time?
A: Running a multinational I hope.

boo.com: Money to burn and nothing to show for it

Financial Times; February 2, 2001
by **James Politi**

If Letsbuyit.com's bankruptcy proceedings hadn't been interrupted in a last minute rescue operation by investors last week, the Dutch-based retailer would have taken the cake as Europe's largest internet failure ever, having burned more than $180m in investment.

But for now, the defining moment of the troubled times in Europe's IT sector remains the collapse of Boo.com last May. Only three months earlier, Boo was being praised as a promising venture and a probable global leader in selling trendy sportswear over the internet.

Riding the wave of euphoria, the London based on-line shopping site and its Swedish founders had managed to secure $135m through private investment.

But come May, the dotcom prodigy only had $500,000 left in the bank, and a cash burn rate of $1m a week.

Since then, Boo has become a potent symbol for all that can go wrong in the new economy. It combined overambition with mismanagement.

Ernst Malmsten, the chief executive, admitted: We were too visionary. Boo attempted to launch in 18 countries simultaneously, while lacking the logistical support to ensure the delivery of goods within days. It also failed to guarantee discount prices on upmarket sportswear and fashion items, giving customers no particular reason to choose Boo over traditional retailers.

At the same time, lush spending, high salaries and technological maintenance costs were eating away at Boo's cash flow. So when its website was finally launched five months late and revenues began to trickle in, the damage was already done.

Mr Malmsten realised this too late: My mistake was not to have a counterpart who was a strong financial controller. But Boo's lack of attention to its accounts was also due to the all-too-convincing nonchalance displayed by investors and venture capitalists when confronted with mounting losses. One Boo investor said that losing $100m was not seen to be important, given that they were building a company worth £1bn ($1.5bn).

Those hopes never materialised. Instead, Boo's downfall had a sobering effect on Europe's IT sector. Furthermore, it demonstrated that ventures are just as susceptible to failure in the new economy as they are in traditional business, if they lack a sound business plan.

In October, Boo was relaunched by Fashionmall.com, the US internet company, as a youth fashion portal.

Its activities will be based initially in the US and the UK, rather than in 18 countries. The new Boo has an advertising budget of $1m, as opposed to the $28m the old Boo could play around with. If nothing else, Boo brought prudence into cyberspace.

There was a let's do something mood in Germany. It was comparable to the mood after the re-unification of Germany. It all seemed very bright.

Bernd Muehlfriedel, Finance Director, 12snap

The entrepreneurial candle, if not snuffed out, is barely flickering. I don't think events have changed people's dislike of risk. This period [of internet boom 1999-2000] has been too short and the evidence of failure is now too ubiquitous.

Diana Noble, Reed Elsevier Ventures

We are still excited by the opportunities of the internet economy. [We] have learned more in the last year about managing a high-growth company than we ever imagined. We have no intention of returning to our old jobs...

Robert Norton, Toby Rowland, Founders of now defunct Click Mango

It is exciting to see the spread of an entrepreneurial culture, where more people are willing to take risks in their careers and do new things. The same thing that has happened in the US in Silicon Valley and Boston is happening here [in the UK]. The key issue is not whether there are lots of failures of individual companies now, but what will emerge in three to five years out.

Marc Andressen

Voodoo says if you are failing – fail fast

There must be two thousand other people in this conference hall and you're all listening to what sounds like the music from **Pulp Fiction...**

And this big black guy comes on stage and the music stops to the sound of guns firing

– guns firing? –

and he says:

Good Morning. Have I disturbed your concentration?

I want to tell you some stories this morning.

This conference is called *Blueprints for Future Success,* but I want to talk to you at first about Failure.

And specifically how our personal and organisational fear of failure – if not recognised, acknowledged and faced – can cripple us.

And the danger of that is that our pasts become our futures...

OK, let's begin. And let's begin with a truism.

The enduring legacy of the internet era will be speed.

Acceleration will not be limited to technology and technological advances, but to everything in business – decision making, growth, product lifecycles and, fundamentally, the lifespan of a business. Time-scales are collapsing everywhere. There is accordingly a prevailing need to execute and implement even quicker. Many organisations are making impressive inroads into this new method of working. New businesses, both dotcom and traditional, are appearing all over the place. One of the truisms of the digital era is that businesses can spring up very quickly in months and sometimes in weeks.

It is also true that they can disappear overnight.

We are now experiencing a dangerous dotcom phenomenon. Failed businesses are not failing fast enough. More importantly, they are not open about their failures.

This is not, I suggest, the case in the USA. Business failure in the USA is seen as a necessary part of learning and subsequent success. American entrepreneurs tend to see their personal standing rise after a business failure – provided of course that they learn from their mistakes. A failure is a 'Purple Heart' or Badge of Courage. It certainly is not stigmatised the way it is in the UK.

British entrepreneurs live in terror of business failure. They have no legal protection like Chapter 11 in the States, where failing businesses are given protection to continue trading whilst endeavouring to pay off creditors. They have to face the spectre of potentially being struck off as directors. They may even face criminal proceedings for trading whilst insolvent. Far more

Voodoo catches you doing things right

unforgiving is the stigma associated with failure. We've all heard stories of businessmen sitting in the park all day with their briefcases, even though they have been made redundant or seen their business fail.

This is not healthy, is it?

But the real issue for dotcoms and their stakeholders is the lack of lessons learnt in the public domain. The UK's failure syndrome is leading to a worrying lack of openness about dotcom shortcomings. Many of the rising tide of dotcom failures are replicating the mistakes of the previous 12 months of failure. In the USA, on the other hand, businessmen openly talk about where they went wrong, and how they could have handled it differently. How many times have we seen failed businessmen in the media sharing their reasons for failure?

Richard Greenbury, Bob Ayling, Freddie Laker or even our friends at Boo or Boxman, no admission of failings at all! It was just bad luck…

This environment of fear is leading to dotcoms only owning up to failure when their funding has run out, NOT when the obvious signs of a failing business are there for any experienced management team to see. It is important for businesses not just to revert to the traditional business measures of success; positive cashflow, top-line growth, profits and a healthy order book – but to voluntarily close down a fundamentally flawed business NO MATTER HOW MUCH of their investors' cash they have left!

Did Boo really have to spend £80m before realising the business could not work? Why did Powernet build up £30m of debt before the alarm bells rang? Did Boxman have to spend £30m to realise their market share was disappearing at a rate of knots?

We are experiencing a real internet recession. Recessions are not to do with global warming. Nor can we blame God. Recessions are man-made. It is time for us to encourage openness and honesty in regard to public failure. We also need to make heroes and heroines of entrepreneurs who have the courage to close down a failed business and return unspent funds to their shareholders. Until then we will always remain years behind the USA in terms of our learning.

Perhaps things are beginning to change; we are experiencing the American phenomenon of the serial entrepreneur: an individual who is involved in the delivery of more than one successful business start-up. These individuals have usually tasted failure at some stage, and no doubt will again in the future. They are not fazed or destroyed by these failures; on the contrary, they are emboldened by these failures. Their real fuel is the fuel provided by their successes. These are the role models for the next generation of business tyros. Richard Branson has not been fazed by the relative failure of Virgin Cola, the difficulties associated with Virgin Trains or, importantly, the abject failure of his People's Lottery bid. This does not mean that failure does not hurt, but that it is being channelled positively.

Who else?

Branson in fact was the role model for one of the modern-day serial entrepreneurs: Stelios Haji-Ioannou of Easy Group, a man moving seemingly effortlessly from success in airlines to success in internet cafés to success in the car rental business.

Voodoo finishes off your sentences

And we could list George Davies of Next, then Asda and now M&S. Philip Green – the man known to his friends as Conan the Barbarian, because "if you get into a fight with him, you'll lose an arm" – moving to win Sears, Owen Owen, Olympus Sportswear, Shoe Express and BHS. His usual tactic, they say, is to pounce on a struggling retailer, shred it into tiny pieces and sell the components at a profit. Now he has M&S in his sights.

So we have some role models. We know what we are looking for. But what do we actually have?

We have the worship of the cult of continuous service.

Have a look at this page from Reuter's Annual Report. And I stress that this is one example I've chosen out of many I could have:

◆ Sir Christopher Hogg	63	14 years	◆ R O Rowley	50	21 years
◆ P Job	58	35 years	◆ D G Ure	52	31 years
◆ J-C Marchand	53	28 years	◆ A-F H Villeneuve	55	32 years
◆ J M C Parcell	53	30 years			

In other words, the average length of service is over 27 years!

Is that a problem in a fast world? Can long-serving leaders throw off the weight of learned behaviour? Time will tell.

Do you see what I'm getting at here? Companies love it when their senior management hangs around.

This is a different manifestation of the fear factor. After many years of service in these organisations, they tend to trade on their experience and knowledge of their business. That's where they say their value is. And that's what used to be valuable in a Slow world.

But there is nothing inherently innovative or stretching about this stance, because there is a massive difference between experience and ability. These directors would be much more valuable to their existing businesses if they left and worked somewhere else, especially in a completely different industry or market, and then returned or perhaps did not! They would see things differently, and perhaps start to challenge the corporate 'sacred cows' and the corporate immune system.

A brilliant example of this is happening at Sainsbury's at the moment. Peter Davies was appointed Chief Executive in 2000, a great homecoming having previously spent 10 years at Sainsbury's, leaving as Marketing director in 1986. During his time away, he was for eight years Chairman of Reed International, the massive international publishing conglomerate. He then went on in 1995 to be Chairman of the Prudential, where he turned around a staid assurance company into one of the leading innovators in its field, culminating in the launch of Egg, the internet bank. The major advertising campaign for the Prudential had Davies' voice giving a human feel to what had been a faceless insurance organisation. It worked massively well. It is notable that just the announcement of his return to Sainsbury's gave a tremendous fillip to the ailing supermarket's share price.

Davies has tasted relative failure in his time. Whilst I worked for IPC Magazines, Peter Davies was, as I say, the Chairman of Reed International, IPC's parent company. He was charismatic and had bags of vision, but he was ousted in one of the many Anglo-Dutch political battles that Reed Elsevier (the merger of Reed International and Elsevier) became infamous for. This disappointing experience has not blunted Peter Davies at all.

Now he has commenced turning around the image and performance of Sainsbury's.

This is a superhuman task. He is clearly the man for the job. He has already sold off Sainsbury's Homebase. He has started bringing in senior talent, and the old guard is disappearing as we speak. One of his most radical thoughts has been to consider moving the head office from Blackfriars to a new building which will not have the association with the old culture and method of working. This is both brave and instructive. Corporate cultures can be so strong as to appear impenetrable, pervasive through all the fabric of the organisation. Change the HQ, he suggests, and you might just give licence to other radical thinking amongst the building's inhabitants.

He has also presided over not just a logo facelift. Not toyed with the brand values, but buffed and polished the rather dowdy brown logo, which really did look a legacy from the 1950s.

But what will be the hardest thing for him to change? The culture. The people.

I worked next door to the Sainsbury's head office for over five years. It was sad to see a once great business nose-dive to its precarious current level. However, let's look on the bright side: they were the easiest organisation to poach quality staff from.

As with all businesses in turmoil, the staff they needed to help turn the ship around are the ones with the courage and foresight to take ownership of their careers and break out.

I took a couple of members of staff from Sainsbury's into IPC Magazines. They embodied the Sainsbury's culture. How they behaved in those early days with me showed me the state of play in that once mighty supermarket – and how it had got into its predicament.

The new joiners to my team were massively disciplined and process driven. They dressed in a similar 'suited and booted' manner, were long-winded, produced carefully managed communication (both written and spoken), which never upset anyone, and always managed to dilute the core message to such a level that it was not worth communicating in the first place. They would spend days drafting and re-drafting simple notes to their team members, when this could easily have been conveyed with a two-minute conversation to the people in the same office. Everything was a set piece, rehearsed to the point of blandness.

As their Director, I was treated with a reverence that was astonishing. They would book meetings days in advance to provide me with sycophantic feedback for a new initiative or a talk I had given. They had bags of integrity, and were diligent hard workers. They struggled with autonomy, and much preferred management roles as opposed to leadership responsibilities.

They were the necessary Roundheads in my world of dashing Cavaliers. In time one of them has become a dream ticket – a rare mix of enterprise and discipline. The other one needs constant reassurance and will always be a first-class manager. Enough said.

Voodoo blocks out noise and helps focus

So what have we learnt so far this morning? Failure is a stigma. And in order to protect ourselves from failure, in order to minimise risk, we behave in ways that, ironically, are going to *guarantee* us failure in the future. We produce what we most fear...

And I just want to make one thing clear: this is not about black and white, good and bad. There are few wholly bad leaders – but there may be leaders made bad by being around at the wrong time for the market.

Voodoo does not see things in black and white

Think of Steve Jobs at Apple – the comeback king. Jobs is the master of innovation, the drive behind the brand. He is a hunter. He is not a farmer. Apple brought back a hunter and it benefited them hugely. But are they currently dipping again, perhaps more now in need of the farmer leader again? Think of BA in the UK who have recently appointed a safe pair of hands, someone who's not bombastic or confrontational – Rod Eddington. Just what they need after the recent upheavals and challenges. But Rod Eddington is not going to be right for all their future. Expand that idea: when do you think Tony Blair, the UK Prime Minister, will hand over to Gordon Brown? After all the vision and the barrel-thumping, maybe thrift and caution, maybe a little piece of dull might win the Labour party the next election…

OK. Great, let's take a little break here so I can grab a little drink of water.

Voodoo picks its moments

So we've heard about how cultures can create an environment which attempts to predict success – but actually ends up creating failure.

What strategies can we employ to avoid this?

What if you bring together a culture which is conditioned only to generate success with one which – well, with one which has less of that conditioning?

After my time at M&S, I decided to move to the highly charged and 'full of fizz' world of Pepsi. I joined Pizza Hut, a joint venture between Pepsi and Whitbread. Chalk and cheese, more sabre tooth and pussy cat.

Working in a joint venture with parents born of different cultures, both national and business, presented the opportunity to live in a world of continuous ambiguity. On paper, this looked like a great opportunity to benefit from the differing styles and approaches to business. Whitbread had many years of knowledge about the UK high street. It had the ability to acquire many high street locations, which would act as the springboard for a spectacular land grab by the domineering Pepsi culture, brand and marketing know-how. In reality this potential has taken a long time to realise.

Pepsico is an aggressive, marketing-led business. They were fast-moving, belligerent and 'growth' was the byword on every manager's lips. Wayne Calloway, the CEO at the time, famously ended a global motivational management conference with the not-to-be-forgotten line: 'Remember, failure is not an option.' It left the attendees in no doubt as to the culture of the organisation. These were not empty words. Unlike Whitbread and many other British institutions of the day, senior management turnover at Pepsico was incredibly high. This was by design, and it worked for them. They were brilliant at assessing which staff would thrive in the high-pressure business cauldron that was Pepsico. They ran assessment centres that endeavoured to replicate the environment that the chosen few would be expected to perform in. Perform is the right word. The whole approach to reward and recognition was all about measurable contribution. A poor quarter, or falling behind the competition, could suddenly spell the end for either a manager or a management team. Consequently, managers were selected for their self-sufficiency, resilience under fire, and their desire to win.

This process of selection meant that the chosen candidates were long on enterprise and dynamism, but fell short on team playing and developing people. This was a management team selected to deliver, and quickly. This led to massively exciting times, and every day management were indirectly taking career decisions. Due to the selection process, most managers never stopped to think about the health hazards associated with this method of working in a state of constant frenzy. This was the 'fire, ready, aim' method of working. The real upside was that nobody looked or policed how one did things: the focus was 'what were the results?'

Whitbread were the polite, paternal and genteel joint venture partners. They were far more deliberate and measured in their approach to business and growth. They had a tradition, and a reputation as a Good Place to Work to protect. They were founded in 1742, and were the elder statesmen of the brewing industry. Unsurprisingly, their staff had many years of service, and had more learned behaviour than was healthy for any organisation. Much in the M&S mould, they rewarded conformance. As a result they had heaps of managers, but very few real leaders. They were epitomised by a 'ready, aim, aim, aim' culture. But they were smart enough to recognise this, and knew they could learn a lot from a joint venture with the likes of a Pepsico.

The Chairman of the time was Sir Michael Angus, an extremely polished and polite elder statesman, who was also Chairman of Boots, amongst other senior appointments. Here was a Chairman who was part and parcel of the 'old boys network'. Many of these ambassadors lacked real passion and hunger for the businesses they were supposed to be leading. What Whitbread needed at this time was vision coupled with ability to lead their organisation to deliver. What they had was years of service to the company.

Some members of the senior management did not come through the harsh assessment centre approach, but were seconded from Whitbread. It was massively obvious to all who the Whitbread managers were. They were high on experience, careful, thorough, but definitely 'on attachment' to Pizza Hut. Most of them made it quite obvious that they hankered for the large and beautiful grazing grounds of Whitbread's many HQ buildings. They found the 'lean and mean' Pepsico approach rather vulgar and unseemly. They also felt bulletproof, because they had very different measurements of success, and years of service were very important to them. The grade of company car, more days' holiday, and points collection towards the inevitable fat Whitbread pension – all of this was paramount.

It was enlightening to watch the mix of Pepsico and Whitbread members of the team behave and interact. One telling example was during the annual pay awards; the Whitbread people would accept whatever was given without a murmur, and would not discuss this with anyone.

Voodoo practitioners punch way above their weight

It was not possible to gauge whether they were disappointed or delighted. Their feeling was that senior management were always right, it was not their place to either reason why or God forbid, argue! The Pepsico staff were the exact opposite: salary letters were opened WITH their peers and they would squeal with delight or be back in your office immediately. They feared nothing. Pepsico's was the prevailing culture at Pizza Hut. It was an aggressive business, with an aggressive board of directors. Whilst it was a relatively small business within the Whitbread empire, it punched seriously above its weight. There were no prisoners – neither competitors nor under-performing staff. Turnover at board level matched the pace of change within the business. On my resignation from the board after three years in the business, none of the board members who had been on the board before me were left. Many of them have gone on to bigger and better things, notably Chris Martin the CFO, who went on to become CEO of Storehouse.

It was tough, but character-forming learning.

The lessons learnt from this experience are twofold. The Pepsico culture, whilst exhilarating, and whilst it stimulated growth in a manner that was quite amazing, had some serious failings. The main failing was that staff only had loyalty to themselves and not the organisation. This meant that whilst most people were highly motivated and fearless, morale was always relatively low. Many people suffered ill health because of the sustained pressure to deliver.

That can't be good.

Whitbread were far more caring and fostered great team spirit coupled with tremendous loyalty from their personnel. However, they were one-paced, polite and would never recognise a tank parked on their lawn until it had blown away most of their defences and returned to base. Even then they would debate what course of action to take, and would invariably decide it was beneath them to engage in an unseemly public scrap.

And that can't be good either...

It reminds me of the difference between morale and motivation. I have always believed the old Roman fleets clearly demonstrated the difference between motivation and morale. The slave galleys used to have hundreds of slaves beneath the decks rowing because their lives depended on it. They would have their very own Mister Motivator who beat time relentlessly with his mallet on the dead-wood timekeeper. They rowed to his incessant percussion. Mostly it would be a steady beat that just totally exhausted them. Anyone who passed out was thrashed awake by the eagle - eyed audit management, who patrolled with bullwhips to the fore. They asked no verbal questions, they just provided performance feedback with the crack and slash of a whip. When they went to battle stations, boy did they get their share of motivation, and did they respond! My insight is that their motivation was at a towering level, but my guess is that the ship's morale was not too great.

Pepsi were great at motivation, but could not spell morale. Whitbread delivered seriously high morale, but could not work out how to motivate. The joint venture should have delivered both in theory, but the Pepsi culture was massively dominant.

OK, I understand that we're going to take a break now and then come back after lunch to have the formal Q&A session. Then we can start applying some of this to your issues.

Voodoo does not see race, class or gender

But just before we go, does anyone have any quick questions or comments about what I've said so far?

You pick up your branded conference pen and, in your branded conference notebook inside your branded conference folder, you make a note:

Fear's bedfellows:
◆ conformance,
◆ management over leadership
◆ arrogance
◆ risk-reduction
◆ the personal pension
◆ personal self-esteem
◆ self-preservation

and then you write

◆ our pasts become our futures

Voodoo starts with you...

The next day you check through 71 e-mails, deleting as you go.

One of them has an attachment which you print out and later take home. You fasten it to the door of the fridge, using the magnet on the framed picture of your children to pin the sheet of paper in place.

It reads:

Taking Risks

by **Osho**

The mind is a coward, for those who listen to it become utterly cowardly. The mind is not an adventurer, it is very cautious. It takes every step with thinking and calculation until it is certain that there is no risk, until it has seen others taking the risk, until it has seen others taking the step and there has been no danger; hence listening to the mind is the most disturbing phenomenon of growth.

When everything is going well the mind comes in and says "watch out!" Because you listen to the mind's fears you stop living. The mind would keep you always the same, never taking risks. Newness is an enemy to the mind, sameness is its friend.

The dilemma

◆ To laugh is to risk appearing a fool.
◆ To weep is to risk appearing sentimental.
◆ To reach out is to risk involvement.
◆ To expose feelings is to risk rejection.
◆ To place your dreams before the crowd is to risk ridicule.
◆ To love is to risk not being loved in return.
◆ To go forward in the face of overwhelming odds is to risk failure.

But risks must be taken because the greatest hazard of life is to risk nothing. The person who risks nothing, does nothing, has nothing, is nothing. You may avoid suffering and sorrow, but you cannot learn, feel, change grow or love. Chained by certitudes, you are only a slave. Only the person who risks is free.

www.thepositivemind.com

Pulling onto the motorway and into the evening rush-hour traffic, you take the cassette tape from its casing, steering gingerly as you do so with your forearms for a moment, and slip the tape into the player.

[Music]

[Female voiceover]
Fear is a vitally useful emotion. It places you on the alert, catalyses your senses and heightens your awareness in the face of danger...But fear's danger signals get muffled when we develop a pattern of denying and suppressing your fears. By not paying attention to specific fear signals, that energy gets diffused into a generalised paranoia, a perennial low-grade alarm fever that pervades our lives...

We need, then, to free ourselves from our old, diffused, imploded anxieties so that we are able to fear what actually threatens our well-being...Fear properly channelled yields wide-awake engagement.
Gabrielle Roth, _Maps to Ecstasy_

[Music swells and subsides]

Fear is a negative wish. The more you focus on what you fear, the more likely you are to make it happen.
Keith Ellis, _The Magic Lamp_

[Music fades]

[Male voice]:

Hello. My name is Thomas James. And I'd like to welcome you to this special recording of my *Living on the Other Side of Fear* personal development workshop.

What is on the other side of Fear? Is it reckless abandon to danger? Or is it what some people call bliss? Perhaps it is that wide-awake engagement Gabrielle Roth talks about at the introduction to this tape?

I'd suggest that it is exactly that – a sensation of vitality, of aliveness, where you are free to act and bring solidity to your dreams. A place where life as an endless possibility opens up for you and...

You press the FAST FORWARD button – hold it down for maybe three seconds, then release it

...We all can understand that the feeling of fear is related to some anticipation of threat or danger. It's a signal, a warning, if you will, regarding issues of personal safety and security.

Consider how you actually experience fear. Think about it for a moment. When you're scared – what happens to you, simply at the physiological level?

There you are, driving along listening to this tape and suddenly a huge truck careers across the central reservation and into the path of your car

– now, if you really are driving, I don't want you to imagine this too acutely, OK –

[short laugh]

But what's likely to happen at that point?

You freeze. You tend to stop breathing. Your muscles contract. Your hands lock tight on the steering wheel, your leg goes rigid on the brake pedal, bracing against the anticipation of the impact.

Indeed we have a phrase in our language, don't we?, which sums up exactly what's going on here – frozen with fear.

Just at the moment when you most need to act, you're quite literally frozen with fear...

You hit FAST FORWARD again.

...in much the same way. Do you ever have those dreams that you're back at college and haven't completed your essay in time? Or that you've shown up for a big exam, and you turn over the page, and you realise that you're completely unprepared for this, that you've done absolutely no revision for it at all? Maybe you didn't even realise there was supposed to be an exam! What other dreams do you have where fear plays a part? I have a good friend, a dear friend – let me tell you she's a very successful trainer who works with some of the top companies in America – who every so often dreams that she's turned up for a major presentation to a major new client.

And these executives are all lined up around the boardroom table, and she's handed out her company's brochure and the Powerpoint presentation is all fired up ready to go. And then she notices that she's completely naked! Can you imagine?

Hey, I don't want you imagining that too much, OK, she's a *very* dear friend of mine....

FAST FORWARD. The tape hisses through the machine.

...and so it is when you feel that success lies solely in your hands, when you feel the weight of expectation, the weight that you tell yourself is yours to bear alone. And when we don't express our fears, when we don't share them, we double their power over us. Because we make ourself into Atlas, superhuman, sustaining the whole world. And we forget our humility.

More importantly, we also close ourselves off from the care, the creativity, the love of other human beings...

Yet under all this ridiculous bravado, this selfish heroism, there is that part of us that is convinced that we are never enough, no matter how we perform, no matter what we achieve, no matter what we earn, no matter what we own. It's never enough...

FAST FORWARD

So take what you are afraid of and imagine the worst possible outcome of the thing you fear. I mean, imagine the very worst. Don't shrink back from it, see it in every detail. Maybe it's death?

So see yourself lying in your coffin, your loved ones around the grave crying. Maybe it's personal injury? So imagine the injury has just occurred, before the medics get to you with the pain-killing drugs. Maybe it's being laid off – no, no one's really afraid of losing their jobs, are they? What they're afraid of is poverty, or the sting of failure, or the sensation of not being able to cope, of being found out as not up to the demands of resilience.

So imagine it. Feel that humiliation. Feel that lack. See yourself living on the streets with your children.

Good. And now that you've faced – up front – the very worst that your fear could bring, let it go and

focus your attention on the most positive outcome!

What, too simple you say? Yes, maybe – simple – but *not* easy. It's not easy to let go of all that fear. But at least you have the option.

OK, so we've named our fear, we've faced up to the worst it could do and left that behind – now on to the Third Power Technique.

The Third Power Technique: stepping out of the comfort zone.

Our comfort zone is partially shaped by life-preserving fears and partially by groundless ones. To become more capable risk-takers, we must move away from the instinctive response to fear and towards the counter-intuitive response. The constructive, though counter-intuitive, response to fear is to acknowledge and accept it. It's important to let your judgement skills override your reflexive responses to the fear of the unknown and...

FAST FORWARD

like a little devil on each shoulder. And what is that little voice in your ear saying? Is it saying 'Do it, do it, you'll never know what benefits you'll unleash – even beyond the benefits you know about now'? Or is it saying 'Be careful, don't risk it, better not even try, go back to what you know'? Because the thing is, that's your own voice. Why not make a choice about who you're going to listen to? Besides...

FAST FORWARD

Hey, maybe you're showing fear to elicit some kind of response from people – from loved ones maybe? I bet you hadn't thought of that?

Well, is there a better way to get their attention?

FAST FORWARD

...all this mean for you as a manager or leader at work? How does the fear of risk show up there for you?

Leaders who consistently perform at a higher level have certain things in common. They are committed to their success, have a passion for their profession, have clear goals and are uniformly more comfortable taking risks than most. Their ability to take intelligent risks is an important ingredient in their success and a huge determinant in anybody's level of achievement.

Suboptimal performers in the leadership arena settle into their comfort zone, fall into endlessly recurring patterns and stop challenging themselves in significant ways.

Learning how to take risks successfully may mean you have to unlearn risk avoidance behaviours you have acquired or been conditioned into by the culture of the organisation. It's the point at which you take self-responsibility and stop thinking and acting like you're a passive victim of the organisation.

Continued success in your organisation – whatever industry it's in – depends on its employees learning at least as fast as the rate of change outside the organisation. This learning often involves taking risks: risks in trying new behaviours, risks in trying something new and unknown, and risks in developing new business processes.

The business world for some years now has been comfortable with the concepts of 'continuous innovation' and of 'learning from our mistakes' – but how comfortable is it with the actual practice? When did you last hear your boss say 'Hey, you have permission to fail here – because we can all learn from it'? Risk is dangerous – personally and organisationally. Try something new and we might jeopordise this quarter's profits. Don't try it and we might endanger the long-term profits. Easier said than done. Who's going to stand up and take that risk? Someone has to stand up, and if it fails, someone has to take the fall.

Organisations are very public places – and very human ones. Success is absorbed into our daily practice, routinised, and forgotten. But failure is remembered and marked against us.

And how do we know if the new way of doing something is actually going to deliver its promised performance benefits? How comfortable will we all be when performance actually gets worse before it gets better – a common side-effect of learning.

How comfortable will we be with the human side of learning – the fact that doing something new inevitably leads us into states of doubt, confusion and discovery? How acceptable is that range of human experience to organisations which have been designed expressly to minimise uncertainty and ambiguity.

I'd suggest that there are two ways forward here. The first is to make the unsafe as safe as possible – in other words to minimise risk.

For example, you could create practice arenas for innovation. But you'd start them up in areas of work which do not directly impact on customer service delivery. So you can innovate in practice arenas to do with performance appraisal, or meetings, for example. And you can innovate where you have the most confidence. So where relationships are strong in an organisation, you could discuss new ways of communicating, of facilitating change, and of facing the unspoken truths. But where they are not that strong, clearly you wouldn't go there. David Campbell, Smith Richardson Senior Fellow of the Center for Creative Leadership in the US, identifies two major organisational blocks to creativity – itself a risky endeavour. One of the major blocks is a 'preoccupation with order and tradition'; the other a 'reluctance to play'. Building the quality of relationships in your organisation gives it the strength and resilience to challenge the status quo – whilst introducing practice arenas, perhaps, allows it a form of playfulness.

The second way forward returns us to what I was saying about uncertainty and ambiguity and how organisations simply haven't been designed to accommodate those states. We have a choice: we can either change the ambiguity, or we can create organisations that accept it. And the latter is the only sane choice. Because uncertain and ambiguous is how life is.

Uncertain and ambiguous is just exactly the way things are.

If you...

FAST FORWARD

...because you'll want to find a reason not to!

OK, so let's do some summing up.

The first part of overcoming anything is acknowledging that there is a problem. So too with fear. Find someone whom you trust and can help give you direction – and confide in them. Communicate about what you want to accomplish – not what you don't want to happen. If you don't know what you want, stop talking and listen to the possibilities from the person who is mentoring you.

Ask questions. The only questions that are stupid are the ones that are never asked. Remember that you do not need to be Atlas.

Now you can move to the Nine-Step plan for *Making it Happen.*

One. You've reviewed your influencing skills – you've mastered the tools of persuasion and communication, the only thing you have for making your dreams a reality.

Two. You've tackled your fear of failure.

What does that sound like?

'I tried it before and it didn't work'
'if I fail, people will think I'm stupid'
'if I fail, I'll think I'm stupid'

That's right.

Three. You've tackled your fear of success.

And we know what that sounds like:

'I don't deserve to succeed (because I've conditioned myself into unworthiness)'
'I don't want to succeed, because actually I like things the way they are'
'I don't want to succeed, because if I do it will bring me new challenges and responsibilities'
'If I'm successful, it will mean more effort and energy to sustain success'
'If I'm successful, people won't give me their sympathy and keep saying "oh I know", "oh you're right" and "there, there, never mind"

Four. You've a vision of exactly what you want to achieve.
Translate that into a benefits package for your customers/audience and then into a 'small steps/how to get there' plan.

Five. You work only on what lies within your circle of influence. You learn from and disregard the rest. And you're prepared to be flexible in your approach, so you arm yourself with counter-arguments, Plan Bs etc.

Six. You've taken feedback from colleagues and garnered advice from 'experts'.

Seven. You've chosen your time and place for taking action wisely.

Eight. If the response is not what you want, you know you will either persevere – with enquiry, creativity and tact – or you will learn from it and let go.

Nine. You know that nothing will happen on your idea unless YOU make a stand for it.

...so what are you waiting for?

> **As you sit in your driveway, first winter frost beginning to layer itself on the lawn, you listen to the tape playing silently to the end of the reel.**

Do Voodoo....

You log on to the FAQ page on www.corporatevoodoo.co.uk

IN A FAST BUSINESS

What of structure?

Structure is important to every business, but do not build in concrete from the off. We have learnt that loose structures NOT based around seniority or hierarchy work best. The key is ease of decision making. At its nadir M&S had herds of directors, executive and non-exec, approaching 20 people at one stage. This was a recipe for doing nothing, there could never be anything like consensus. Small, fast-moving agile leadership is the best structure and as flat as is sensible.

What of strategy/strategic action?

The by word in fast businesses is good enough strategy, not the precision engineering of yesteryear. The inspired thought will need some embellishment and consideration, but do not give it to that working party or that committee. Put it into action!

The e-business era has taught us that we cannot predict some outcomes, like the behaviour of a new entrant who responds to your new strategic thrust. Be loose, be decisive, be quick, and be ready to respond if necessary. Do not take two years to gestate the initiative, and remember, if it starts to fail, fail fast.

What of networks/information flow?

Most traditional 'slow' businesses are steeped in securing corporate information. It's like a secret society. Seniority tends to be the key to the corporate information vaults, more passwords than are safe for any budding Fort Knox. This is not the way to engage the thinking and ideas of your people, who can contribute masses to corporate initiatives, if only they were asked, or had access. I clearly remember M&S only allowing the chosen few to have access to e-mail, as they were petrified that an external person would be able to access their e-mail system. Well that's the whole point of e-mail, it is not meant just for a few people, the benefits come from universal access. Don't be afraid to speak, be proud to share. This is the first step to unlocking your corporation's knowledge management!

What (other) resources?

In a fast business one of the most discernable differences from traditional businesses is the desire and ability to partner with other organisations. This is two-fold, firstly, they are good at bringing in the experts in areas where they do not have the inherent expertise. The other rationale is when entering a new market or discipline they increase speed by partnering or defray cost/risk by partnering with organisations who are in this marketplace already. Slow businesses tend not to trust anyone or arrogantly believe they can do it better, and consequently take an age to realise that they cannot.

Fast businesses are also very good at bringing in talent at senior levels from outside. They do not just utilise their own gene pool, which usually means someone having to learn 'on the job'. They like external people with knowledge and fundamentally the appropriate culture for this new initiative.

What of competition?

Fast companies always have a healthy respect for their competition, and are prepared to work with them if the market opportunity is big enough, or acquire them if necessary. Vodafone are a great example of partnering with a competitor to enter a new geographic marketplace, or buying a controlling stake in one of the leading players in a marketplace.

What of knowledge?

The acquisition of knowledge is normally done through recruiting big hitters with knowledge of the marketplace they are trying to get into. Sometimes it's easier to acquire an organisation. Fast companies tend also to be well represented at industry seminars and symposiums. They tend to provide speakers who will talk up what is being done in their organisations. They are brave in this respect, but also very smart. this approach of speaking on very public platforms gives them the opportunity to attract the best talent and suppliers who may well not have heard that this organisation is active in a new area. It is also great PR. Slow businesses are usually either too cautious to participate or too arrogant.

Voodoo brings peace and conflict

What of customers? CRM? Customisation?

Fast companies really do engage their customers on a regular if not real-time basis. They see customer feedback not as nice to have but THE essential ingredient in shaping their product and service offerings. They also know that in an increasingly competitive and fast moving world, today's CRM can be tomorrow's obsolescence. CRM is more a state of mind than it is a slick bit of software or methodology. Systems can sure make a difference, but only if great customer service is in the soul of the organisation first.

What of markets/market share?

The fastest of businesses have great antennae in their marketplaces. They are rarely caught unawares, and have great tentacles through their suppliers and customers that keep them appraised of new developments. They tend to be early movers on new initiatives, but will discard them just as quickly if they start to fail.

Market share is no longer a great measurement of success. Quality market share is a much better and harder measure. Having 80% of a low margin and diminishing marketplace is not the place to be. Many Slow businesses are great at managing decline. It is far better to be great at managing growth.

What is this e-commerce thing really?

E-commerce is simply the bringing together of buyers and sellers online. This will be a vibrant marketplace in the near future, but it will not suit everyone. Running a chain of high street stores does not suit everyone, so why should e-commerce, but nearly everybody scrambling to the net would have the 'bolted on' e-commerce bit. Most organisations who scrambled to the net last year, had never sold anything anywhere before. What inherent buying, selling, inventory etc. skills and experience did they have? I think we all know the answer to that now.

E-business is here to stay, but e-commerce is but one relatively small part of the bigger picture. More and more e-businesses are setting up and many are succeeding, but they are playing to their organisations' strengths. Is it any surprise that Tesco is by far the UK's best online grocer? They have clear market-leading strengths that lend themselves obviously and easily to selling online.

How can we get the most from the net?

Focus on your core competence – what is it that you do well above all other things? Nike doesn't make trainers – its competence is in branding and marketing. What do you do well? Is it product and service leadership – your R&D and innovation? Is it operational excellence – order fulfilment, perhaps, or manufacturing? How about customer intimacy – are you best at giving great experiences to your customers in terms of service? Or is it, like Nike, your brand – the marketing and product management skill you have?

Having identified your core competence (and though you have to do bits of all of the above, there'll only be one of the four that you are pre-eminent in), now you can out-source your noncore functions. Rely on strategic partners to do that work. Support this new eco-system with information, and nurture it with trust (together, of course, with some shit-hot contracts, SLAs and measurements!).

In this sense, out-sourcing emerges as a strategic business process.

But the ultimate goal is then to partner with people and organisations who do not have or do what you do. That means you can expand your offerings, your reach, your power…

How should we think about the people thing?

In any big new project or initiative, you'll find three types of people. There are 'the believers' - those who you can be sure are fully on board with the effort. Then there are 'the doubters'. They'll agree with your objectives but may still be unsure about you personally. The doubters need time to come round – and a tight rein in the meantime. The third group – 'the diehards' – are the easiest to deal with. They go immediately.

What about the mavericks? Fast organisations can spot the 'loose cannons' who are comfortable with ambiguity that new, rapid start-up initiatives have and are recruited for the initial fire-up stages. The more solid and management types tend to be brought in a little later when the hunting has stopped and the farming-type activities start to emerge.

Frankincense, Myrrh and Voodoo

The few leaders that survive in companies are not well noticed in slow hierarchical-based organisations. They are actively searched for and nurtured in fast businesses. These businesses will have fast-track programmes and will not be too worried about building elite cadres and pushing them to the top rapidly. The best managers do not necessarily make the best leaders. Leaders can come from the most unorthodox roots.

What is the leader's role?

There are four main aspects:

(i) motivating your people – mentoring them so that they grow, listening hard, passing on what you've learnt, encouraging the team to stretch themselves. One question you should regularly ask in appraisals is this: 'what risks have you taken?' If they're not taking risks, they're not stretching themselves or the organisation. Be a leader who models risk-taking and accompany that with genuine support of others' risks, both psychologically and in terms of rewards. Fully expect failure to happen sometimes: but don't tolerate people hiding their mistakes from you.

Encourage your team to talk about what it has failed on so that learning can happen and so that you can act to limit the damage. Thus:

(ii) providing air cover – concentrating on making the best of things when things go wrong does not minimise the fact that failure has repercussions. One organisation's great learning opportunity is another organisation's lost revenue. So when they go out on a limb (or maybe too far out),you should be there to provide the necessary air cover. Even the most empowered business has its elements of politics. Use your political clout on behalf of those who have none.

(iii) selling the organisation's capabilities – your audience for this selling is, of course, customers, but also shareholders, suppliers, the media, potential partners, investors, potential buyers. And, of course, your people need always to be convinced that the organisation is worthwhile of their investment and has a compelling future. If you're running a department rather than a whole company, sell to the board level usually. Go anywhere you're needed. Be mobile and very visible.

(iv) attracting talent – all of us are in competition for the best talent. You need to be abundantly clear as to why a talented person would want to work for you – what's the value proposition as far as they are concerned? What sort of talent do you need where in the organisation – and when? What do you do to develop talent – in other words how do you help them maintain their brand as a talented Individual? And does everyone in the organisation see it as their job to attract, retain and develop talent?

You do Voodoo

And then your computer says:

Your connection has been discontinued for lack of activity

E-mail to CEO

Frank,

When we get together in San Francisco next Monday, you've allocated me an hour's slot to talk about the future of our marketplace. I've taken it upon myself to expand my brief. I thought you'd better have notice of some of the points I'm going to be making during that session.

Here they are:

15 BIG QUESTIONS I'LL BE ASKING THE BOARD AT OUR SENIOR EXEC'S RETREAT IN SF

1) How different are we? What is our uniqueness – and where does it show up: in our products, in our services, in our route to market, in our ideas creation? In the questions we ask of ourselves?

2) We are always asking 'what have we done last week, month, quarter, year?' But I want to know 'Who are we?' What is work for – and how is our answer to that question reflected in how we treat our people? What is an organisation for – and how is our understanding of that purpose reflected in everything we do?

3) Or do we just operate on someone else's answers to those questions?

4) Where do we want to be? Coca Cola own 50% of the cola market, but only 2% of the consumable beverages market. So are they big or small? What do we want to be? Is that ambition clear to all our stakeholders?

5) How human do we sound to our customers, to our people? Or do they see us as just another corporation trying to push our brand, just another organisation trying to buy their talent?

6) Who do we value and why? That guy in my team with the Limp Bizkit on his DVD player and the tape over his eyebrows because we've made a 'no way' judgement on his piercings: he's the best thing that ever happened to my team. I used to think it was just because – despite how he looked – he was still a good performer. Now I realise that because of how he looks he's a symbol that we're an open house for talent – no matter what form it takes. That's important.

7) Why is this company in love with itself? It came into the new economy on the back of a great wave of optimism, of "can do", of the new cool. And half of us fell in love with the product, with the tools, with the code and half of us fell in love with the possibility that we might make a million each. And no one fell in love with some old, true principles, such as that customers matter a bit. There's a big 'Us!' in this company, but not a big enough 'You!'

8) We have stopped creating this organisation – now all we seem to do is run it. We've become managers, all over. When I recruit someone, I'm trying to find people who will take this company forward after we're long gone – I'm not trying to find people who'll repeat its past on my behalf.

Voodoo is the only means necessary

9) What of significance have we done recently other than sell the Chemstor brand? Which was the last opportunity we pursued? Which the last efficiency we optimised? I know which was more recent.

10) When did one of our board meetings – hey, when did any meeting in this company – value imagination over rationalisation, 'what if?' Over 'who did..?'

11) When did you last talk with rather than talk at our people at the Friday beer bust?

12) When did we last have some customers walk about our site, walk through our processes, give us some advice?

13) Why is this company dead? Why is it only an org chart and set of financials? Where do we measure its connections with people, with customers, with partners?

14) When was anyone in this senior team stretched as opposed to just being busy? What are we doing in the field of leadership development? What on earth did Belbin and Myers Briggs do for us? What did the three MBAs we sponsored bring us beyond a raised salary bill? What skills, capabilities and perspectives are we missing for the sorts of ambitions we ought to be setting ourselves?

15) Why do we keep strangling our strategies to death through analysis, debate, research and fear? Why do we keep believing that we'll find this killer way forward which will be perfect? And why do we keep losing opportunities whilst we're trying to design perfection up front?

Why don't we act with courage and go for a good enough strategy that we can trust itself to improve on whilst we're doing it?

That's it. Those are the fifteen. I thought you should be aware of how strongly I feel.

By the way, I've given up my fear of what you'll think of me now that I've said these things.

Frank, I'm looking forward to a robust discussion next Monday.

Have a good weekend.

> ***The following Friday morning. In the plane, as you stand waiting for 'doors to manual', your Palm bleeps and you flip open the cover to see a message waiting.***

Daddy

It says

Here's what I did today
◆ I flew over tall buildings
◆ I fought the bad guys
◆ I ran around really fast
Miss you, come home soon

You tap the Reply button.
Write:

So did I!

Miss you too

I'm almost there

And send the message home.

In the airport bookshop, ten hours of jetlag inserting warm, hard fingers under the muscles in your face, your mouth a mix of metallic gut juice and airline-strength breath freshener, you take a paperback from the shelf – the title and author's names flash briefly out of a deep black cover – and you flick through the pages...

...the people who don't have access to a corporation to which they can offer lifelong loyalty are the majority. And for young workers, consistently overrepresented among the unemployed, part-time and temporary sectors, the relationship to the work world is even more tenuous. – No Logo

And this...

*Because young people tend not to see the place where they work as an extension of their souls, they have, in some cases, found freedom in knowing they will never suffer the kinds of heart-wrenching betrayals their parents did. For almost everyone who has entered the job market in the last decade, unemployment is a known quantity, as is self-generated and erratic work. In addition, losing one's job seems much less frightening when getting it seemed an accident in the first place. We begin to wonder...why we should depend on the twists and turns of large institutions for our sense of self. – **No Logo***

You put the book back on the shelf and head for the exit.

Back in the office – only a security guard populates the place at this hour – there is a handwritten note from your best employee – your 21-year-old star employee – propped up against an empty Pepsi can on your desk.

It says:

Hi again.

You asked me to reconsider the resignation letter which I brought to you last week. I can't do that. I've done all my considering and reconsidering over my decision. You also asked me, in your voicemail last night, to help you understand more about why I'm quitting. That I can do.

Voodoo thinks big and acts small

I think it's only fair. I don't believe in this company any more – if I ever did – but I do believe in what you've been trying to do over the last eight months.

Remember when they brought in that work/life balance counsellor a couple of months back? She was good, wasn't she? At any rate, she really helped me to think through some things, get some things clear. I don't know if she did the same for you. But it became easier for me to speak about things which I'd always guessed you weren't supposed to talk about. Like just how pressurised and complex my life is. I look around at my friends and those who aren't my friends and we all seem to be trapped in this mentality that says if you're having fun, if you're being successful, if you've got the right clothes and the right gear and know the right clubs then everything's cool. And there's this thin film separating the me that lives and works in that world where everything's just fine - and from that place it is, because from there I've got a great life - and the me that lives and breathes in this world where I'm only just holding myself together. There's the me that's got all the stuff - and this job has allowed me to get lots of good stuff - and the me that knows it's all pretty worthless. I shut the door at night and there's only me, you know. Even when I'm in a relationship, it's easy to think of the boyfriend as just part of the same stuff.

Remember that article you passed round last year - from that magazine, I can't remember its name. Brand of You or Brand You or something. I get it - I do it well enough. But does it always have to be about me, about the individual? Me Inc. What do I have? What do I need? What's my grade? What univ did I go to? What salary do I earn? What do I wear? Because after a time, you find yourself thinking who's got what I want? And who else has got something better than me? You can get sucked into this comparison thing. And we do it at the same time as knowing how superficial it is to do it. And how do you think that feels? 'Cool, beautiful, clever and self-contained but please don't let me down'.

Have you ever read *American Psycho* by Brett Easton Ellis? Pretty fucked-up book, in a way. But it's about this guy who's killing all these girls in some disgusting ways, and at the same time he's always preening around; he loves himself. The book has these long sections which are all about what beauty products he puts on his skin in the morning and where he buys his shoes. I guess it's a satire about appearances and reality, you know? Well last week in the weekend paper there was a feature on male grooming – and one of the young guys in there was inspired to start making himself look good by that character in *American Psycho*. That's so shallow (but he looked good too).

So I shut the door at night and there's only me, as I say. And all the advertising tells me that I can have what I want, be who I want, have it now. I sometimes wonder whether I'm supposed to think that the Brands are all I need to know. That the 97 channels on my TV are all I need to have to be entertained and educated. And other times I just feel that I'm surrounded by a pretence of choice.

Why bother to leave the house? The TV and the web are my friend and family at the end of a remote or a mouse. Lonely Planet is my buddy in a book. And when I do leave the house, I sit alongside all my colleagues at work staring at a computer screen all day (or once a week we gather in the restaurant to watch a web-broadcast from our esteemed CEO in LA). Or we go to a bar every night and check each other out – with all the headaches and hangovers that ensue from that. That's why I love clubbing. At least there, when you're dancing, you don't actually have to watch anything...All this attention we're paying to someone else, something else, somewhere else. It's like watching someone else take a call on the train at night going home - they always seem to have much more fascinating mates on the other end of the line than ours. Do you know what I mean?

I once read someone describing what I'm talking about here a lot better than I am doing now: they said we were in danger of becoming tourists in our own lives...

But what's all this got to do with work, and why I'm leaving. I don't know. What would I say if I did know? I'd say: that I'm desperate for some recognition, for some acknowledgement in my life - and I don't feel I get any at work.

How am I doing? Dunno. Everything's moving so fast, changing so quickly that I lose track of what I'm being compared against. Where am I headed in my work? Dunno. The timeframes are always so short, that we're always just focusing on what's right in front of us. So there's always a buzz around the place - all that energy being expended has got to produce a buzz, right? – but what it all adds up to, I'm really not sure. And I'm even less sure if it makes me feel good any more.

And yet I'm doing well, aren't I – that's a good chunk of money going in the bank every month. I daren't even tell my parents what I earn, they'd be astonished, appalled. Am I doing well? (Posh and Becks are doing better, right?) Everything's always telling me that everything's always possible, everything's always within reach, that I can have everything I can dream. My mum tells me what it used to be like in her day, how I've never had it as good. And sometimes that feels more like a very big weight of expectation, rather than a freedom or a release.

Maybe it's because we never get a feeling that we're completing anything at work. We work on the Yaboya.com account, and even though it's a great success, it never feels like we ever got to the end because by the time it does reach some sort of finish line, the original account team are all split up and working on other things by now. How many celebrations for projects were there last year? The only thing I can remember passing the champagne round for was new business wins. Something new to start working on...

And I know what you were trying to do when you chucked out the appraisal system. You were trusting us. You were treating us like adults, giving us more freedom. You can assess yourselves, you said. You're all mature enough to know how well you're doing, what you should be developing. And you can assess each other. But it's hard to get the pitch of self-criticism right when the workplace is like I'm describing it here. I never feel I can praise myself too much or too loudly. There's always a next challenge. I'm never sure where the imaginary mark is. How good are my communication skills? How good is the team at communicating? I don't know about them, but I don't like the way we're always just that far from snapping at each other. But I'm scared of being snapped at, or taken the wrong way – or shunned, I suppose – if I really say what I feel.

And how good are you as a leader? I think you're trying to be a great leader. But I rarely see you, because you're always flying between meetings, or I see you getting pressured from the top. Or running around trying to deal with the latest gripe about something probably petty from somebody like me, maybe. Or fighting to get us our bonus on time. Is that what leadership is?

Voodoo is the goal scorer never the goalkeeper

So, how do I feel about work? Almost OK, almost worthwhile, almost exhilarating. And at the same time, almost out of control, almost crazy, almost overwhelming. How do I feel? Almost fine. And almost disillusioned. Default setting for emotions: faintly miserable.

What a pain I must be sounding. I've just read through all this again and a) it's not coming out like I intended it would and b) Jesus, I sound so pathetic! I should cheer up, huh? I've got lots to be happy about. The apartment, the job, the friends (who I love, by the way). But they never taught us how to be happy at university. They just assumed we'd find out for ourselves I suppose.

My Dad has God – he's a CofE supporter – and I have *The Matrix*. He had *Patton* and *Reach for the Sky* and I've got *Enemy of the State*.

So, again, why am I leaving? I remember when you wrote me that letter of recommendation when I was up for that promotion last year. What did you say I had? Humour, thoughtfulness, a passion for what I do, direction and self-motivated ambition, self-confidence, an ability to enjoy myself and be happy, and 'a large capacity for taking more interest in other people than herself'. And that's why I need to move on, to try a change of direction. Because, in fact, underneath it all, too often I feel pretty much the opposite of all those things: neurotic, cowardly, dull, directionless, exhausted, miserable, and self-obsessed. It's time to get things even clearer, to sort out where this is all heading. Three years ago I came into this industry saying that I was going to work flat out for five years and make a fortune. I'm on my way to that fortune. But now I feel too tired for that, too tired of that. I've got to find out if there's anything more durable and meaningful to focus on. Do you think there is?

So first of all, I'm going to take some time off, some time away. I'm 23 next year and I feel like I've had my foot to the floor since I was 11 years old.

Thanks for all you've done. Don't take this personally. You're doing a great job.

> **Later...**

> **You order another large Tanqueray and tonic and a Peroni for your friend.**

> **And you say something like**

"*ivvegotagdet*"

> **You take another drink, breathe deep and attempt it again**

"*I've got to get out. I've got to leave.*"

"It's not the only option, of course." says your friend, putting the Peroni to his lips, "Though it's the obvious one when we feel we've lost our power".

"*I'm full of power – that's why I've got to go.*"

Voodoo is both old and new

"No, you're full of anger, but your power is trapped, it's given up to others in your company. You're part of someone else's strategy, someone else's reality of beliefs and decisions. It's not unusual – lots of people accept that as an inevitability. They see it as accepting reality. Because they have to have a job to pay the mortgage, they think it's fine to lose themselves, offer themselves up on a plate to the organisation. So that when they hit a low, or when frustration peaks, like with you now, they can excuse any amount of pain by saying "hey, I'm not in control" or "My Boss did it". See yourself as an employee and you'll create that paradigm in your life. The limits are up before you start."

"Outside is better."

"Whether you're outside or inside, you need to take your power. Freedom is what you crave, but there's freedom inside companies too – as long as you ensure you're living your own plan. What is the driver for your life, what is your goal? When you're driving the plan, the organisation may become an ally or a necessary stepping stone rather than a shackle."

"Outside is still better. They used to call people who worked for themselves self-employed. Then they called them contractors. Now what do we call them? Free agents. Free agents."

"Outside there can be slavery too. How many people who work for themselves end up working more hours not less, working harder not easier, locked into feast and famine mode? Scared to turn away work when they are busy, scared it'll never come again when they're not. And outside you'll need to be very good at knowing when you've done enough. In the organisation, if you do well, they put you up the hierarchy, up the pyramid, and like in any pyramid, all the lines point to the stars. And they'll do that to tell you how marvellous they all think you are. And outside, without all that external acknowledgement, you'll need to be very strong at avoiding the trap of never feeling good enough. Can you accept yourself as you are?"

"No, because I'm not where I want to be."

"Good. That's the start of a life driver forming – finding out what your vision is. But you'll never be your vision. Ever. There's what you dream you can be, and then there's always you, where you are, good bad or indifferent. The difference is the creative tension that keeps you alive and growing. And you are always doing the best you can given where you are at the time, given the context you're operating in."

"So I should change the context and leave."

"You can change the context without leaving. Who are you and how do you choose to operate?"

"I want to be happy and successful and loved."

"Aw. That's nice. In that case, you'll have to work on those things that are in you that make you unhappy. Otherwise you'll carry them around from job to job and never change anything."

"It could be argued that inside you're protected from yourself. Scared of saying how you feel, scared of telling the truth? No worries – invoke your political power and you can sidestep the need for conflict. Scared of facing up to yourself? Great. Ask for some feedback from your junior

Voodoo does what it says on the can

staff. They aren't allowed to tell you the truth, so you'll never hear it. Always putting off the important actions? No problem. Get busy in a committee for change – there's no shortage of ways of looking like you're really involved."

"Outside, maybe, you'll have more opportunity for self-reflection. Away from the noise of organisation, with fewer other voices chattering around you, telling you what you want to hear, there's a strong chance you'll learn to trust the voice inside your head. Your intuition, whatever you want to call it. The one who tells you the truth. And being so much closer to your mistakes and successes – I mean, having fewer layers between you causing them and you feeling their effect – you might well be able to learn from both your successes and your failures."

"But all that's possible inside an organisation too, if you make it happen. You'll have to be someone who stands for honesty and integrity. And you'll have to tell everyone about it, about what you'll tolerate and how you'll be acting. Do it and you'll create it, even where the organisation didn't have it before. Don't do it because you think the organisation won't change and you'll never have it. And therefore you won't be happy."

"Accepting a salary doesn't equal accepting inevitability. Businesses of any scope, size or nature only die when their leaders give up."

"That's easy for you to say. You're already outside."

"Learned behaviour is hard to throw off, whether you are in or out of a company."

"Sorry?"

"Listen, let me tell you a story that shows you what I mean."

"IPC Magazines. Remember? The largest consumer magazines business in Europe. Loads of market-leading titles like *Loaded, Marie-Clare, Country Life, TV Times.* An organisation over 100 years old, with huge heritage values. Most of its readers would not recognise the IPC Magazines name, but they are very loyal to their particular title or brand, whether they were into dogs or boobs or soaps."

"In the 1980s they used to call IPC the Ministry of Magazines. You couldn't challenge its status. It had a relatively high cost base, but before the introduction of sale or return to the wholesalers and retailers, there was a licence to print – literally - money. But the advent of sale or return removed protectionist and penalising costs to the retailers and wholesalers, and demanded significantly better controls. A new style of leadership took over the company, and was prepared to take some really tough decisions with the organisation, and cut huge swathes through both costs and sacred cows. Profits soared, and the organisation started to attract some serious talent, both in journalism and management."

"At this stage IPC was still a wholly owned subsidiary of the publishing conglomerate, Reed Elsevier. Reed Elsevier was moving to become solely a business publisher. This made tremendous sense, as the margins were so significantly higher in business publishing as opposed to consumer publishing. This unwritten strategy made for uneasy feelings at IPC. Nevertheless, the IPC management continued to deliver record profits each year."

Voodoo is more than mere magic, it's your magic

"Now, there were many advantages to having a large, powerful parent who had no intrinsic interest in your business. Whilst enjoying the safe position as a subsidiary, IPC were effectively left to manage the business in a near autonomous fashion. As long as the results remained good, both parties were happy."

"But the markets became a deal healthier in the early 1990s, and IPC magazines started to experience some heavyweight competition. The usual suspects were still there: EMAP, National Magazines, Condé Nast, Haymarket and the rest, but now there were lots of new, small, agile fast-moving competitors. These guys were no respecters of heritage or scale. They smelt blood."

"By the time IPC eventually realised that it too needed to respond, it found itself hampered by the past. Cost cutting – much needed at one time - had become second nature. This was an organisation that was expert at being prudent and thrifty, but had forgotten how to nurture growth. It was a situation obviously encouraged at Reed Elsevier. There would be no support from them for a sustained period of investment in the organisation."

"End of chapter one of my story."

You order another round of alcohol from a waiter who you see to be shaking his head to himself.

"Chapter two begins with what looks like a new world. The markets are experiencing Mergers and Acquisitions on a scale never experienced before in the history of business. The deals are getting bigger and bigger, management buy-outs and leveraged buy-outs are becoming common at first in North America, and they had now arrived in Europe."

"Enter the cavalry: a whole band of Venture Capitalists chasing quite voluptuous returns which could be made by buying slightly under-performing companies and assisting them to grow prior to a flotation or a trade sale."

"IPC Magazines fitted the bill perfectly. A move away from Reed Elsevier would not only allow the management to become masters of their own destiny, it would provide the incentive for the organisation to grow rapidly, and raise the finance through a quick Initial Public Offering to dominate its marketplace."

"During 17 heady days spanning Christmas 1997, the deal was done, and IPC Magazines became the highest LBO in the history of the UK at £860 million."

"In January 1998 the business celebrated Independence Day. A new world, a new order, a new strategy and the same management! As a board of directors, we…"

"*OK*"

you say

"*I thought you might be connected to this somehow*"

"Yeah, I gave it away. As I say, we were euphoric. The strain of working long hours together for 17 days with a common goal had made a team out of us."

"We knew the exhilaration of liberation. Inside an organisation, you see – and apparently free! This coupled with the fact that we were now part owners of the business as well. It was exhilarating stuff! By delivering the growth the investors required to make their investment worthwhile, we would march to the stock exchange for flotation, or to a bidder who wanted to assist in the long-term growth of the business. Everything in the garden is rosy…"

"Now, about those targets we agreed with the investors. We knew they were tough. We also knew that the 'experts' setting the targets had minimal understanding of our industry. Everyone got caught up in the frenzy of escape and a life transforming transaction. We signed up willingly."

"The sales line and the profit line needed some serious and significant oxygen. It needed that oxygen at a pace we had never experienced before. The euphoria of the night before soon turned to a morning-after focus and seriousness."

"And how did that focus and seriousness assert itself? In our learned behaviour. We had been number one or two in many of our served magazine markets. Our culture was one of preserving market share, not aggressively growing it. Management at senior levels had grown up in a culture of cost cutting and consequently their learned behaviour was characterised by some quite defensive attitudes and approaches."

"Board meetings became ever longer. Board agendas focused on the problems and issues in the business – never its growth or strategy. The culture of management became audit focused: ensuring staff did what they were supposed to do with ever diminishing resources to do it with."

"What happened to liberation? Where did the Promised Land disappear? Did we take a wrong turn? Should we go back? If only we could…"

"Then we started getting feedback from the organisation. The major one was their desire for more and more communication. The board, on the other hand, thought that we were communicating well. In this brave new world, fear is everywhere, and we were the living embodiment of that fear. We were under pressure and showed it. Putting a brave face on things was not the way forward. Our behaviour was increasingly transparent. And our financiers had replaced Reed Elsevier. They had transformed in our eyes from being the cavalry to guards of the prison gates."

"But – and here's the message to my story – the problem was ours not theirs. We were naïve and had grossly underestimated the task of turning around the prevailing culture. The board started to disintegrate. It seemed that every couple of months another board director would go. So we cut costs again."

"We could not break out of the old Voodoo."

"And so you left. So should I."

Voodoo sometimes hurts, but always cures

"Well, as for me, I realised I'd lost focus on my personal goals and became intoxicated with a dream that I now realise was not really mine. But had I found that my personal goals were aligned with building a business of that sort to that end – then I could have stayed, and worked with it. Many left IPC but many also joined. Bring in new and fresh talent who exhibit new fast qualities and importantly have no baggage – that's how you can turn a culture around."

"But in the end the incumbents need to give the insurgents their heads. That might ultimately mean them standing aside. You are only able to take that huge step if you have no fear. And, I guess, if you really love your company."

"Great leaders have no fear and love their organisation more than their egos."

"I still think outside's better."

"Look, there's no inside, there's no outside. There's only where you are. There's no life and work and family and health and whatever to balance. There's only one thing: life."

"Hey, look, you have a choice. Either you could stay and act courageously. Or you could be courageous and go. Does that sound like good advice? Does that sound like a choice?"

"Come on, drink up. You're looking…tired."

Your friend helps you into the cab, and tells the driver how to get you home. You see your friend take a couple of notes from his wallet and pass them over. The taxi driver reaches over and switches off the meter. The red numbers fade to black.

"Take care of yourself"

your friend says.

The cab moves gently away. Tomorrow, you know already, you will regret the hangover.

But you will not regret your decision.

You even share it with the taxi driver, just to be sure.

And when, next morning, you do wake up – in your familiar bedroom in your familiar bed with your familiar partner beside you – you find in the inside pocket of your crumpled jacket a piece of paper, a print-out from a web page.

Voodoo is always there for you, if you want it

Seven Reasons we are Black

An essay by **Michael Finley**

There must be something wrong with me, because when I got my census form last week, I dutifully filled it out. That is, until I came to the section marked race. On an impulse, I said that our entire family was black.

We aren't ostensibly black. One look in the mirror confirms that. We are white as sheets, the four of us.

But I did it anyway, probably committing a felony in the process. I can't tell you what the no.1 reason was. But I had my reasons, and I will list them here, in no particular order:

1. First, the question bugged me. What do we say about ourselves when we check off a box like that? If you know nothing about me except that I'm white, or that I'm black, how does that help you understand me? In fact, doesn't it have the opposite effect — painting me with vague, sweeping probabilities that may or may not be true?

2. I did it out of plantation liberalism, a hard habit to break. What good it will do is unclear to me. My understanding is that the census exists primarily to count citizens so that congressional districts may be accurately apportioned. But what our color has to do with congressional district apportionment is, again, a mystery. Also, minorities get undercounted in the census, and are thus underserved in government outlays. So I thought I'd counter-balance an uncounted black family with our family. Sure, this means fewer benefits for my race, but I figured, Hey, white people had a good year.

3. I always wanted to be black, like in the Lou Reed song — it's more fun, would be the sanitized reductio. And this seemed like a much easier and more socially acceptable way to go about it than wearing makeup like John Howard Griffin in *Black Like Me* (1962). And less embarrassing than Al Jolson in *The Jazz Singer* (1929).

4. I thought it would do my family good. I told my family at supper we would be black from now

on. Not that it would change anything in the way we go about our business. But somewhere, on a government mag tape database somewhere, spinning around at a bazillion miles per second, we're black. My family didn't care.

5. I wanted to show solidarity with my extended family, which is diverse, including great people of numerous stripes and hues, including African-American. To my in-laws Kathy, Seantelle, Neecie, John and Marcus — this is for you. And to my Uncle Jack, who used to do audiovisual work for Jesse Jackson, and now has a huge adoptive family of folks of color — I haven't met you all, but I can tell you're terrific.

6. Patriotism. If I have heard anything repeated over and over all my life until it makes me sick, it is that you can be anything you want to be in America. You can be president, or an astronaut, or a cowboy. Well, at the moment I want to be black. So by what right can my country bar me from this ambition? I know this sounds silly, but I mean it. Isn't this the place that isn't supposed to put a ceiling on your ambitions?

7. Because, scientifically speaking, we are African-American, and so are you. According to the Eve Theory, which is more than just a theory, the entire human race appears to have originated in the DNA of a single woman who lived on the Olduvai Plain 1.5 million years ago. Every living person has DNA that can be traced to her. If that doesn't make us African, what could?

And the banner ad at the top of the print-out, in colours of red and purple and white, says CANADA CANADA CANADA.

Though this means nothing to you, it does make you smile.

Epilogue....

In the eyes of Westerners in the 19th Century, any element of African culture smacked of barbarism. In Haiti, the agitators who emerged from the [slave] rebellion of 1791…were used as proof of a connection between voodoo and savagery. The same apprehension was invoked in the 20th Century to justify the American occupation of Haiti in 1915, turning the island into a land of the living dead.
Voodoo Truth and Fantasy, Laennec Hurbon

Anyway, you give someone this [puffer fish] poison, often by blowing it in their face, and you can't detect their breath or heartbeat. They're buried immediately because of the heat, then the witchdoctor comes along at night, digs them up and blows a hallucinogen in their faces. The shock jerks them out of paralysis. But it also gives them a trip. That with the cultural impact of knowing about zombification, blows people's minds and reduces them to being zombies.
Robert Twigger, *Independent on Sunday,* 11 February, 2001

I put a spell on you…
Nina Simone

Up in the plantation house, the slave trader stands in front of his own altar…

So after all this time, dear reader, there's a complication. We have a secret to pass on.

Initiates of Corporate Voodoo create Fast businesses. We hope that by now you've some insights into how they do it. But Muggles are not the sad, sleepy, harmless giants you might imagine them to be. Here's the secret: even Muggle organisations already practise their own Corporate Voodoo.

REPEAT: EVEN MUGGLE ORGANISATIONS ALREADY PRACTISE THEIR OWN CORPORATE VOODOO

But it's not the same as the one we've been talking about in this book. And they've been doing it, secretly, for so long, that no one realises that's what happening.

The Corporate Voodoo practised by Muggles is a spell, a curse, it's what keeps people there, what neotonises them, what makes them into zombies.

It is what keeps people in check, keeps them faintly motivated but mostly disillusioned and hopeless.

It is what breeds powerlessness.

It is the thing that has produced the shared hypnosis that work is a curse.

It is what creates total dependence on The Organisation for both mortgage and self-esteem.

It is what convinces people that they have no future beyond this job.

That the greatest fear in the world is losing their job.

It is what tells them there's no point in being innovative, because 'they' won't listen; it's what creates an environment of collective self-disempowerment.

It is what restrains creativity and subversion, because those things are difficult to control. One doesn't want the slaves thinking for themselves...

Working for some organisations is like having the puffer fish poison blown in your face. It blows your mind.

Beware this Voodoo. It is a mighty powerful spell.

Your choice? Personal Voodoo is what gets you out, puts you back in control, releases the magic.

Initiates can then create Fast businesses, if they have the Personal Voodoo.

But Muggles keep the magic out of the conversation.

Reader, we exhort you: get paranoid! Wake up from the spell!

It's in the house, the magic's in the house...if you would but see it...

So, what is this Personal Voodoo?

Personal voodoo — the gateway to a magical life

Whilst Corporate Voodoo will make a tremendous impact and difference for organisations that are brave and progressive enough to take this on and really embrace it, the real difference it can make is to you! All organisations are made up of a collection of individuals who in progressive organisations have a common goal or purpose. Organisations change in units of one; individuals, people. It is important to kick off with a personal plan for change, which can be used as the template for your organisation.

Phase 1. Manage your Personal Voodoo

It is imperative to have a real driver for your change initiative. It's rarely sustainable to catch a bit of inspiration or an insight into what you are unhappy with, and to use this as the fuel for sustainable change. There will be many obstacles and disappointments *en route* to the change you are after.

The best initiation process is to produce a very simple plan with the 4-6 things you want to achieve over the next three years.

STOP NOW. WRITE THEM DOWN HERE.

THE OUTCOMES THAT WILL DRIVE MY LIFE OVER THE NEXT 3 YEARS ARE:

HEALTH WARNING:

IF YOU CAN'T WRITE THEM DOWN, THEN YOU'RE LIVING IN SOMEONE ELSE'S VOODOO

Your life drivers need to be simple, personalised, achievable and, importantly, measurable. You have to know when you have got there. They could be as simple as owning your own property, or perhaps as complex as starting your own business. They need to be goals that will excite and inspire you, and will be life-transforming when achieved. They need to be challenges of the sort that will force you to focus.

The first and most positive change these life drivers will have on your behaviour and emotional well-being will be that they will greatly assist you when those inevitable small hiccups occur throughout your life. Usually, you will be able to focus back on your goals and not feel sidetracked, and be able to rationalise the fact that you were overlooked for that promotion, or the personal loan you applied for was rejected. These life drivers will bring you the necessary adrenaline needed to succeed.

Because they are personalised you will not forget them, and you should have them indelibly printed on your mind, and it will be so much more powerful if you can envisage what the world will look and feel like if you get there. These pictures will become more vivid as you get ever closer to delivering them.

Voodoo creates a vibe in the cinema of the mind

Pictures are fantastic fuel for your everyday engine. This fuel and the visual experience will create an overwhelming desire to get there and soon. This addition of hunger will start to generate pace, which is the vital ingredient. It will not be all right on the night, unless you get there and get there quick. If it is that important and can deliver what you are after in your life, why would you want to be patient and really measured about this? Become necessarily impatient with standing still, feel the exhilaration of getting closer to your goal. Take the time to catch yourself doing something right. Build your own self-esteem and morale. Take hold of your career and your contribution, feel the liberation, and enjoy your success.

Voodoo says: accept your inevitable freedom; don't give it away

Some would have us believe that we are in the midst of a revolution. We may well be. However, this does not require a call to arms. It's more like an escape to victory. This is a world brimming with the ability to free ourselves – to live your personal voodoo. But first we need to disconnect ourselves from the chains of an older Corporate Voodoo.

For many business generations we have increasingly had our careers planned out for us by well-meaning managers (or were they?), who inherited their method of working from the Corporation's unwritten operations manual for people. Their theoretical support was the the human-relations movement in the 1940s, which encouraged companies to focus beyond extrinsic motivators such as salary to intrinsic motivations, such as working conditions and workplace relationships, in the belief that a fulfilled worker – not just a well-paid one – was most productive.

The talent war is not a new phenomenon. The desire to recruit and retain the best available staff is long-established. In a competitive environment, most smart organisations started to realise that working conditions and complementary salary packages could really build staff loyalty and thereby retain the talent they need for as long as possible, if not their whole career.

This paternalism – and this word is not too strong to describe the dependence mentality some old-Voodoo corporations create in their staff – led to many encouraging features of the 1970s and 1980s rewards systems:

◆ subsidised meals for all staff

◆ interest-free loans for management

◆ discount vouchers for all staff to redeem against the company's products and service

◆ share schemes for staff

◆ save as you earn

◆ benefits for personal well-being which have been expanded into the modern age by increasingly talent-hungry firms, from subsidised hairdressing to reflexology, from chiropody to laundry, from meditation rooms to Fun Centres.

This has led to the most amazingly low attrition rates for staff. In some traditional companies, staff turnover was measured by fractions of a percent. Is that a wholly good thing? Maybe, from the organisation's perspective (that's their Voodoo) But the adjacent problem is that many people could not afford to go. Before long many members of staff became hugely reliant on their package or perks. They had to stay.

The initial goal of achieving loyal staff who really did believe in the organisation was definitely achieved. The secondary goal of retaining staff was also achieved. Another less obvious, long-term and unforeseen goal was also surreptitiously delivered: the inexorable rise of a conformance culture, where serfs became unknowingly sycophantic to these generous Lord and Masters. Slowly, they stopped challenging and thinking, and just did what they always did, endeavouring to perform in a manner that management would notice and reward with promotional points and gold stars. New ideas and challenges to the status quo were seen as damaging to one's perk-potential. So individuals made the conscious or unconscious decision to exclude such behaviours from their style – and thus, inevitably, from the corporate culture.

Voodoo always lives together before, or instead of, marriage

The syndrome of employment as ghost-marriage is a great danger to one's personal Voodoo. For better or for worse, for richer or poorer, staff stay on and on, not daring to imagine, let alone attempt, the single life again. This slow paralysing of thought, innovation and empowerment wreaks havoc in time on any healthy organisational system – and on the personal system.

We all need to learn from this. Create and establish your own goals and your own road map for your own success. Utilise your own measurements and terms for success. Start feeling good about your contribution to your life goals. Involve those around you that you want to care for and want to care for you. Build your own personal eco-system that will support, contribute to and benefit from your growth.

And, most importantly, see your organisation as a temporary partner in your life but not the means and the ends of it. Your company is a momentary co-creator with you of development, growth, learning, fulfilment, meaning and wealth – not the source or benefactor of those crucial things.

This mind-set, funnily enough, will reciprocate your organisation's real thoughts about you…

Voodoo lives a life of interdependence

Remember the best partnerships are those borne of interdependence, not dependence or independence. You will be amazed how positive this can you make feel, and how important your own eco-system will become to you. If you have chosen well, then you can start to feel the feeling. There is nothing so transforming as an unconditional positive response (UPR). Normally, our children and loved ones are the only ones who care enough to deliver this. Think a little wider; whom else are you sharing with? Who else needs something from you, and what do you to give to them?

He that always gives way to others will end in having no principles of his own.
Aesop

If you don't like something, change it. If you can't change it, change your attitude. Don't complain.
Maya Angelou

He is able who thinks he is able.
Buddha

It is no use saying, 'We are doing our best.' You have got to succeed in doing what is necessary.
Sir Winston Churchill

Phase 2. Identify your own Personal Sorcerer

There is no better feeling than knowing you have your own personal trainer or mentor. Being the Sorcerer's Apprentice can be massively rewarding, if the Sorcerer is a person of great wisdom and standing in your eyes.

There are three steps in the process...

Step One

Identify the traits you would really like to have. Establish how you would like to be seen and remembered.

STOP NOW! WRITE THEM DOWN HERE.

**The characteristics, qualities, values and behaviours that
I would most like to live by are:**

HEALTH WARNING:

IF YOU CAN'T WRITE THEM DOWN, THEN YOU'RE LIVING IN SOMEONE ELSE'S VOODOO

Step Two

Now identify which person that you know of demonstrates that behaviour as a matter of course. Hopefully, this will be someone that you know or know of, and perhaps a friend of a friend, or a colleague of an acquaintance.

STOP NOW! WRITE THEM DOWN HERE

The Quality	The Sorcerer for this Quality
1	....
2	....
3	....
4	....
5	....

Step Three

Now approach these people. Ask them if they will be your mentor (your Sorcerer). It may sound impossible to achieve, or a huge imposition to ask of someone: but remember we all have egos, and most people will be flattered even to be approached in this way. Most Sorcerers will want to have their spells live on.

Nelson Mandela said recently in London that 'unsolicited advice is rarely listened to or respected. But solicited advice is treated with due care and attention, and creates bonds that are rarely broken or forgotten.' Great Sorcerers can share many years of learning, wisdom and experience in a very short space of time, if the apprentice has the ability to listen, hear and act on the ingredients and recipes that are being shared.

Voodoo is rarely written learning, it is handed down from generation to generation, sometimes through great war stories, feats of derring-do, fables and some great contemporary urban myths. Sorcerers paint vivid pictures that are easily kept in one's mind's eye. Bob Marley called this his ' Natural Mystic'. It is this Natural Mystic that does not fit with conformance cultures, but is the oxygen of your personal Voodoo.

Know why you've chosen them

The choice of Sorcerer needs to be taken seriously, and you must aim as high as you can. Ideally, your prospective Sorcerer should know you or of you, but this is not essential. They must be someone that you inherently respect and look up to. Their position and knowledge should be aspirational for you. There should be a significant gap between their experience and wisdom and your own.

Ask for what you want

You will feel that they are too busy or important to give up their precious time for you. Do not let this feeling put you off at all, rather think how wonderful it would be if they *were* your personal mentor. Once you have settled on a short list of three or four people, make contact immediately – there is no reason to wait. It is helpful to go through a common acquaintance to broker a meeting, but this is not essential; just make contact.

Make it easy for them

All you are asking for is an hour or two every couple of months. Offer to perform all the necessary legwork to make the meetings happen; organise all the meetings, preferably in their office (to make it easy for them), prepare any agenda or discussion points in advance. It is important to stress the confidential nature of these relationships, and that nothing said in the meeting would be mentioned outside. This is imperative to enable the mentor to feel at ease. Offer to try one and see how it goes for both parties. The only measure of success is that the two parties want to keep on meeting. It will just die if either party is not benefiting from the relationship. Remember, Sorcerers can pick up a trick or two from their apprentices, sometimes just the confidence and pride the relationship can give off is return enough. The real drug for the Sorcerer is to be involved in the growth of precocious talent.

If at first you don't succeed, be all the more determined next time around. The benefit of being a mentee is seriously worth a couple of rejections to get there.

Phase 3. Make up your own empowering principles

So, finally

– though we sincerely hope not –

we at Voodoo always promise our clients that we will give them the Ten (or so, depending on their situation) Golden Ingredients that will guarantee transformation in their organisations.

We tailor these ingredients to them. They are bespoke. Otherwise they would be Not Golden.

We don't know you, reader, but in our travels we have probably met people very like you. So until we do meet you face to face, here are the **Ten Generic Personal Voodoo Principles** that we urge you to consider and draw on:

1. Consider: How does what you do improve your customers' lives? People want their lives to be better – easier, smoother happier, more peaceful, richer – than now. Can they get it elsewhere? The more they can only get it from you, from your own unique fingerprint on your product or service, the more they need it.

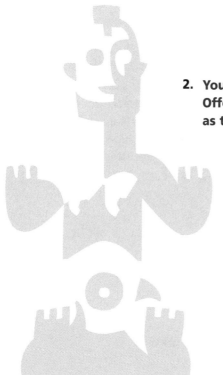

2. **Your customers always want more than you think they do. Offer wide as well as deep. Change to match your customers as they change.**

3. You must hire help who will expand the promise beyond you, not replicate it on behalf of you. That requires fearlessness and love on your part.

4. **Above all, people (your staff, your customers) seek meaning.**
    Give them a meaning (a goal, a purpose, a calling, a promise).

5. Deliver. Make everything you imagine real.

6. Nothing can be done well on your own, even masturbation. How rich is your network of influences, mentors, capabilities? And how rich is their network? That sum is how rich you are.

7. **Delve deep to find out what really makes the difference, for you and then for others. Focus there.**

8. **Connection is a promise in a lonely world, a tool, and a process. You have to keep working at it. You have to put in to connection with your customers, your people, your self, what you dream to get out.**

9. Change the world by all means, but you'll only know how to do that by having an intimate and constantly updated understanding of how it currently seems to work – what currently seems to drive it, and what it appears to be lacking.

10. **Never fool yourself that things will always tie themselves up into easily memorable prescriptions, or that promises will come true. Life's a mess. Adapt. Make it up.**

You'll always learn another equally powerful insight, if you listen.

The Liturgy

Voodoo loves new age financial engineering

Voodoo is risk-embracing

Voodoo loves virtual

Voodoo accepts uncertainty. Whatever...

Voodoo is customer-led

Voodoo is not: closed-cultured

Voodoo knows a bit of Latin
(radix [radical] = root)

Voodoo hates jobs for the boys

Voodoo is not: product-obsessed

Voodoo is not: physical

Voodoo is never: deeply cautious

Voodoo lives beyond the curriculum

Voodoo loves maths; Voodoo loves dance

Voodoo lives and works in the neighbourhood

Voodoo works on all levels at once:
   the Voodoo is in the system

Voodoo looks beyond the first impression

Voodoo experiments in order to create

Voodoo loves immediacy

Voodoo connects in order to create

Voodoo says: important but not sufficient

Voodoo distrusts old measures

Voodoo takes a stand

Voodoo likes a nice surprise

Voodoo hates blandness

Voodoo gets together

Voodoo says: consensus is no way to run a company

Voodoo does not see things in black and white

Voodoo picks its moments

Voodoo creates a vibe in the cinema of the mind

Voodoo says: accept your inevitable freedom;
    don't give it away

Voodoo always lives together before, or instead of, marriage

Voodoo lives a life of interdependence

Voodoo is suspicious of the neat and tidy answer

Voodoo loves the mess

Voodoo inhabits harsh reality
and Voodoo inhabits the dreamworld

Voodoo asks: why clarify the contradictions?

Voodoo asks: do you know what you're doing?

Voodoo asks: are you thrilling yourself today?

Voodoo asks: why predict the future when you can make it?

Voodoo asks: how radical are you being this year?

Voodoo says: the fundamentalists haven't heard the
good news yet

Voodoo challenge: write your own most compelling story about you

The Voodoo is not in the cornflakes

Voodoo asks: how are your strengths your weaknesses?

Voodoo asks: when was your last life-changing moment?

Voodoo says: take care of yourself

Voodoo disturbs the way things are

Voodoo celebrates

Voodoo is not found in the kitchen at parties

Voodoo values the buzz factor

Voodoo listens to the [corporate] fool

Voodoo asks: in what way would the company have to change for your value to be maximised?

Voodoo accelerates education and wealth

Voodoo asks: in what ways should you be fearful of yourself?

Voodoo warns: who you are is your future

Voodoo embraces the new rules of attraction

Voodoo connects to a powerful future

Voodoo believes differences are creative

Voodoo is bored by sameness

Voodoo says choose. Then choose again.

Voodoo says if you are failing – fail fast

Voodoo catches you doing things right

Voodoo finishes off your sentences

Voodoo blocks out noise and helps focus

Voodoo practitioners punch way above their weight

Voodoo dose not see race, class or gender

Voodoo brings peace and conflict

Frankincense, myrrh and voodoo

You do Voodoo

Voodoo is the only means necessary

Voodoo thinks big and acts small

Voodoo is the goal scorer never the goalkeeper

Voodoo does what it says on the can

Voodoo is more than mere magic, it's your magic

Voodoo sometimes hurts, but always cures

Voodoo is always there for you, if you want it

Voodoo is both old and new

Voodoo says sequels are a good thing,
  except when they aren't

Voodoo asks: what's in Voodoo Two?

Reader, if you know what should be in Voodoo Two, tell us...

◆ if you have ideas, suggestions and experiences of living the Voodoo Life, share with us

◆ if you want us to come and spread the Voodoo message in your business or community, invite us

◆ if you want to talk with us about the Ten Golden Rules that will really transform your business, call us

◆ if you could bring together a group of truly influential people, from whatever field, to discuss the Voodoo message over a specially convened dinner, nominate them

◆ if you can imagine an empowering theme for our global webcast on 31 October, 2001, name it

Voodoo gets involved

www.corporatevoodoo.co.uk

*For if death is unavoidable – the universal outcome –
outplaying it with life lets one face it successfully.*

Postscript

Music for reading by: The Voodoo Chill-Out Mix

Music and rhythm are at the heart of Voodoo. In our work with clients at The Voodoo Group, we make great use of sound and lyric. *Corporate Voodoo* is remaining true to this heritage: our Voodoo CD has been compiled to provide a complementary and conducive environment in which to read the book.

Tracks we listened to whilst making this book include:

Prior to picking up the book (again)

Traveller (Kid Loco's Mix)
Talvin Singh
on *Cafe Del Mar Volume 6*
MERCURY RECORDS

In The Air Tonight
Phil Collins
ATLANTIC RECORDS CORPORATION/
WEA INTERNATIONAL

CHAPTER ONE
Initiates create Fast business

Angel (Club Mix)
Ralph Fridge
2000 CONTINENTAL RECORDS/
MINISTRY OF SOUND RECORDS LTD

Fire Starter
Prodigy

Move On Up
Curtis Mayfield
IVAN MOGULL MUSIC

X-Factor
Lauryn Hill
EMI MUSIC PUBLISHING/
BMG MUSIC PUBLISHING

Three
Massive Attack
ISLAND MUSIC LTD & SONY MUSIC LTD

CHAPTER TWO
Muggles live in Slow business

Wake Up Everybody
Harold Melvin and the Bluenotes
V.CARSTARPHEN/G.MCFADDEN/J.WHITEHEAD/
B.MARTIN
(FROM *WAKE UP EVERYBODY*)

Zombie
The Cranberries
from *No Need to Argue*
ISLAND RECORDS

That's Life
Frank Sinatra
POLYGRAM INTERNATIONAL PUBLISHING

It's All In The Game
Van Morrison
XR PUBLISHING

Time Will Tell
Bob Marley

I Know What I Know
Paul Simon
GENERAL MD SHARINDA/PAUL SIMON

CHAPTER THREE
Towards a Voodoo world; honour the children

Wide Open Space (Perfecto Mix)
Mansun

CHAPTER FOUR
Voodoo embraces everything

Be As One
Sasha and Maria
POLYGRAM LTD

Faith
George Michael
G. MICHAEL – SONY MUSIC PUBLISHING

Lifted
Lighthouse Family
POLYDOR UK LTD

Walking On The Moon
The Police
EMI BLACKWOOD MUSIC INC

Mack The Knife
Frank Sinatra
HAMPSHIRE HOUSE PUBLISHING
CORP./ASCAP

Lion In Zion
Bob Marley (Remix)

CHAPTER FIVE
Voodoo is not afraid

Bullit (Main Theme)
Lalo Schifrin
WARNER CHAPPEL MUSIC LTD

No Man is an Island
Rebel MC
FICTION SONGS LTD

CHAPTER SIX
Voodoo starts with you

Breathe (Cygnus X remix)
The Art of Trance
PLATIPUS RECORDS

Natural Mystic
Bob Marley
ISLAND RECORDS

Praise You
Fat Boy Slim

CHAPTER SEVEN
Do Voodoo

The Band (Way Out West Remix)
Marco Zaffarano
TRANSIENT RECORDS

Haitian Divorce
Steely Dan
MCA RECORDS LTD

Californication
Red Hot Chilli Peppers
WEA/WARNER BROS

Lucky Man
Richard Ashcroft

Epilogue

Revelation (Ferry Corsten remix)
Electrique Boutique
2000 CONTINENTAL RECORDS/MINISTRY
OF SOUND RECORDS LTD

Push Upstairs
Underworld
from *Everything, everything*
JBO LTD

For details of how to buy the Voodoo CD, visit www.corporatevoodoo.com

Acknowledgments

We live in a fast-moving, information-rich world where content bombards us on all channels, every day, for ever. This book is a symbol and a product of such a world.

We gratefully acknowledge the following sources:

Page v   West African Dahomean Vodoun: Historical background http://spiritnetwork.com

Pages 5 & 6 Taken from www.nando.net/prof/caribe/origins.html and http://www.geocities.com/Athens/Delphi/5319

Page 8   Chris Decker from *Return to the Source* www.rtts.com

Page 12   [Dr Erica Weir, CMAJ 2000;162(13):1843-8]

Page 15   www. justpeople.com/content/leaders/ leaderdb/chrisgent.asp

Page 16   Interview with TWST.com

Page 19   Hans Snook, Orange Renegade source: ft.com Hans Snook…faded hippy © 2000 Reuters Ltd.

Page 20   The Orange…flop ©Associated Newspapers Ltd, 14 February 2001 Orange founder Hans… Guardian Unlimited ©Guardian Newspapers Ltd 2001

Page 21   Branson in dress... www.stepstone.co.uk

Page 22   Virgin Territory… *Newsweek International,* June 19, 2000

Page 25   Tesco corners… source: Ft.com

Page 26   All companies that are successful… Extract from speech by Terry Leahy Chief Executive Tesco, British Chambers of Commerce Conference 2000

Page 31   The idea that certain…Robert Palmer, *Rock & Roll, An Unruly History,* HarmonyBooks, New York, 1995) The arrival of African slaves… Louise Tythacott, *Musical Instruments,* Thomas Learning, 1995 African based drumming… Palmer *ibid* Today's drummer… David Tame *The Secret Power of Music,*

Page 32   One simple guideline… posting on Hong Kong Association of Christian Music Ministry Web Site Harry Potter www.exposingsatanism.org/ harrypotter.htm

Page 45   All change on Oxford Street… *The Independent,* Robin Stummer and Hester Lacey 25 February 2001

Page 50 NatWest signals defeat
The Independent, AP 11 February 2000

Page 54 BT dials old boy network…by Chris Ayres
The Times 26 September 2000

Page 57 Muggles, Fascinating… from *The Harry Potter Lexicon* www.i2k.com

Page 58 The lives of many kids… Jean G. Fitzpatrick, essay on beliefnet.com

Page 60 London – The Studio has been set up… originally an article by Steve Tice on http://www.nycfame.com/innercircle/film/88TVFromLAToLondon.htm

Page 66 *E is for e-education* originally published in E-biz

Page 72 Extracts from *All Our Futures: Creativity, Culture and Education:* a major report on the future of education by the National Advisory Committee on Creative and Cultural Education (NACCCE). With permission

Page 77 *You Can Make a Difference for Kids* published by 3M and Search Institute 1999 www.search-institute.com

Page 79 Extracts from 3m.com

Page 82 Re-inventing Diversity:… originally written for HP's *The IT Journal*

Page 122 *Taking Risks* by Osho… found at www.thepositivemind.com

Page 123 Fear is a vitally useful emotion. Gabrielle Roth, *Maps to Ecstasy,* Thorsons

Fear is a negative wish…Keith Ellis, *The Magic Lamp,* Three Rivers

Page 146 The people who don't have access…from *No Logo* by Naomi Klein, Flamingo

Page 147 Because young people tend not to see …from *No Logo* by Naomi Klein, Flamingo
Hi again. You asked me to reconsider the resignation letter… Thanks to Dr Nick Baylis, Research Director of younglives.com for the inspiration for this passage; younglives.com is research project into the concerns and hopes of people aged 16-25 in UK today

Page 164 *Seven Reasons we are Black*… For more of satirist/social commentator Mike Finley's writing, visit him at http://mfinley.com

Thanks also to Viv Craske at *MixMag* magazine

If we have inadvertently failed to recognise a source, we apologise unreservedly and promise to put it right in the next edition or volume of this work.

René and David would like to thank David Butler and Jeremy Hughes, who were early storytellers in the Voodoo mythology, and all their supporters in the Voodoo, Carayol Ltd and Treefrog Ltd teams.

May God and lwa bless all at Capstone and Andrew at Baseline who made it look like this.

Appendix

Towards the end of the writing of this book, David received the following in a mailing from Tesco. It struck us that only a supremely confident Fast business with no shortage of the Voodoo spell in them would produce anything as smart, sassy and fun as this as part of its recruitment campaign…

One less thing to bother about...

TESCO

So you're getting offers. Loads of them. We know and you know it's because you're in demand. So why settle for anything but the best?

To save your valuable time, we've enclosed a letter. It's for you to use – to turn down all those other hopeful businesses.

But remember – they won't like being out-manoeuvred by us.
So be kind.

For an offer you can't refuse, get in contact now. And here's how.

Executive Talent Team
Salisbury House, Bluecoats, Hertford SG14 1PU, UK

Tel: +44 (0) 1992 510506
Email: 506@hodes.co.uk

Insert here the name and company of
anyone other than Tesco who makes you an offer

Print your address here

Dear *(please insert recipient's name)*

It is with regret that I won't be accepting your generous offer.

Well actually it isn't. In fact I'm very happy. Smug even. I've been offered a position as Change Consultant in a company that loves ambitious high achievers like me; a groundbreaking pioneering giant of a business which will push me and set me on a track that's faster than, well, yours.

It's not that I'm unhappy with the package you offered. This is just a much better deal for me. And I don't want to rub it in, but they are the UK's largest, most successful retailer, with a record for growth and innovation I won't find anywhere else. Did you know that their Dot.com portal makes them the world's biggest on-line grocer? Oh, and I bet you didn't think their biggest store would be in South Korea. Think of that next time you notch up your Clubcard points.

Anyway, that's the kind of environment I'll be soaking up. Success breeding success and all that. A variety of challenges stretching across the business – food, non-food and beyond. And talk about impact: I'll use my experience and MBA knowledge to drive through radical change projects that even your Gran will notice.

And the company? Tesco of course. Don't worry, there are plenty of people who didn't quite cut it; I'd be happy to point them your way. Thanks again for your offer.

Yours sincerely

(please sign and print your name)